AF240882

Understanding Plotinus

Thibaut Gress—Sébastien Barbara

Understanding Plotinus

Introduction:
Plotinus or the Exemplary
Life of a Soul

Biographical and Historical Overviews

Little is known about Plotinus' life. Most of what we know about him comes from the biography Porphyry of Tyre (234-310) dedicated to his master, entitled *Life of Plotinus*[1], which he wrote between 300 and 301 as an introduction to his edition of the *Enneads*, the name given to the writings of Plotinus assembled by Porphyry. The paucity of information we have about Plotinus' life can be

---

1. We refer systematically to the edition of Plotinus' *Treatises* edited by Luc Brisson and Jean-François Pradeau and published by Garnier-Flammarion from 2002 to 2010. Porphyry's translation of *Plotinus' Life* is appended to *Traités 51-54*, Paris, GF, 2010, pp. 259-316.

explained by the context of the time, but also by his own philosophy: singularity is not the end of a life, and in this respect, the challenge of philosophy is rather to rediscover the universal meaning of reality than to lose oneself in the details of the particular. If a life is of any interest, then, it is in a very specific sense, and not the one promoted by individualism, which supports the idea that each life is interesting in itself, because it is lived; on the other hand, if it makes sense to evoke the life of Plotinus, it is only because *the philosopher's life must be exemplary; it is not captured in its chronology, nor in its acts or episodes, but by the example it sets.* The philosopher's life is not of the order of what was once called a "chronicle"; it is an example to be followed, the object of a qualitative presentation, through which he shows and, consequently, indicates the most worthy behavior—which is why the only virtue of a biography is *ethical.*

Moreover, the philosopher is characterized by his separation from the normal world of men, he has a singularity *as a philosopher* and not *as an individual, which* Jean-François Pradeau sums up very well in a remarkable introduction to the philosophy of Plotinus: "the philosopher, like a god among men, is the one whose admirable, if not miraculous, gestures are remembered[2]."

In all likelihood, Plotinus was born in 205, in Lycopolis (Upper Egypt), then part of the Roman Empire and where Greek culture was alive and well, probably into a family of high-ranking Roman officials. In this respect, Plotinus' culture is complex: as an Egyptian, and therefore as an eastern citizen of the Roman Empire, he must have spoken Greek, a language also spoken by the Empire's elite. Plotinus was therefore a Hellenophone in two respects: he was one of those who, having received a good education and coming from the East, considered themselves to be Greek in language and culture. Nonetheless, Porphyry points to a rather approximate use of the Greek language, both spoken and written.[3]

---

2. Jean-François Pradeau, *Plotinus*, Paris, Cerf, 2019, p. 15.
3. "[…] he made mistakes when speaking […], and he pronounced other words with mistakes that were found in his writings", Porphyry, *Life of Plotinus*, 13, 3-5, *op. cit.*, p. 292.

At the age of 28, Plotinus went to Alexandria to study philosophy with the Platonist Ammonios Saccas, known as Ammonius, a spiritual guide of Christian origin (perhaps an apostate) whose teaching was purely oral and left no written records. Virtually nothing is known about Ammonius, but we do know that he opened a school in Alexandria, attended by Origen[4] ; Plotinus attended classes from 232 to 242, where the rule was to say nothing about what was taught; this was certainly esoteric training for spiritual advancement according to very demanding rules, about which an oath was taken to say nothing: Plotinus eventually broke the oath, which caused quite a stir.

At the age of 39, in 244, his interest in Eastern—i.e. Persian—and Indian philosophies[5] led him to join the

---

4. Cf. on this subject: Jean-Michel Charrue, "Ammonius et Plotin", in *Revue philosophique de Louvain*, quatrième série, tome 102, no. 1, 2004, pp. 72-103 and Richard Goulet, *Porphyre, Ammonius, les deux Origène et les autres*, in *Revue d'histoire et de philosophie religieuses*, 57e année, no. 4, 1977, pp. 471-496.
5. Olivier Lacombe, "Note sur Plotin et la pensée indienne" in *École pratique des hautes études, Section des sciences religieuses,*

army of Gordian III, the Roman emperor (238-244) who was marching against Persia. The defeat of this army and the death of Gordian, killed in 244, forced Plotinus to take refuge for a time in the city of Antioch (now Turkey)—an operation that was not without its difficulties.

Plotinus then moved to Rome, then under the reign of Emperor Philip the Arab (244-249), where he gathered a number of disciples to form a philosophical school which, in modern times, became known as the Neoplatonist School of Rome. Contrary to popular belief, this location may come as a surprise. Indeed, Rome was not a hotbed of philosophy at the time, as it was much more readily distributed between Alexandria and Athens. It was therefore the imperial court and senate that brought Plotinus to Rome, for reasons more related to power than to the institution of philosophy as such. We also note—and we'll come back to

Annuaire 1950-1951, 1949, pp. 3-17 and Joachim Lacrosse, "Plotin, Porphyre et l'Inde : un ré-examen", *Le Philosophoire*, vol.41, no. 1, 2014, pp. 87-104.

this—that the role of women was already important, in that in many respects they played the same role as the Parisian salonnières of the Grand Siècle and the Enlightenment: Plotinus thus met Salonina, the enlightened empress (254-268) and wife of Gallien, as well as the aristocratic Gemina, wife of the future emperor Trebonianus. It was thanks to the protection of women that Plotinus was able to establish his school in Rome. It follows that Plotinus was not a hermit, but a man of the court; Porphyry's account contradicts the image of the isolated philosopher, the reclusive sage withdrawn from the world; Plotinus was practically a courtier, and seems to have realized the usefulness of associating with power.

A school is not a school of thought, nor is it something to be taken in the sense of "making a school" with the idea of a clear doctrine shared by all members; a "school" of this time has something of the mundane about it, again like modern salons: they are informal, irregular meetings of educated people, seeking essentially to progress ethically. A clear distinction must therefore be drawn between, for example, teaching of an esoteric—and indeed partly doctrinal—nature, as might have been the case with Ammonius, and "schools", which are more akin to more or less open, socially mundane circles.

These clarifications help to determine the general meaning of Plotinus' philosophy: it cannot be reduced to treatises, or even to teaching that is not sufficiently doctrinal; rather, it is a *way of life*, a kind of propaedeutic of an ethical nature. Porphyry writes to emphasize this dimension of Plotinus, and illustrates Plotinus' example whenever he deems it necessary: "When he spoke, it was the intellect that manifested itself even on his face, which he illuminated with his light[6]".

This is no mere detail: it helps us to understand that philosophy can only exist if we go beyond ourselves, and if the practice of thought enables *us to become more than ourselves*, or, more precisely, *to become more*

---

6. Porphyry, Life of Plotinus, 13, 5-7, *op. cit.*, p. 292.

than an individual engrossed in his or her particularity. Philosophy therefore only has practical meaning, as a "way of life[7]", and its effects must be visible on the philosopher, who therefore becomes exemplary. This is why Plotinus refused to allow his portrait to be drawn, his birthday to be celebrated, his individuality to be celebrated. All that matters is "conversion"— etymologically, the turning away from the particular and the material towards the essential, the universal and the unchanging. In simpler terms, we could say that conversion—*epistrophê* in Greek—constitutes the fundamental requirement by which we *turn away from the real to rediscover reality*, i.e. by which we turn away from material multiplicity to rediscover the fundamental structure of this multiplicity.

From 254 onwards, Plotinus agreed to write texts taken from his lessons, which Porphyry would group together under the title of the *Enneads*. The lessons dealt with a difficulty identified in Plato's dialogues,

---

7. We refer to Pierre Hadot's famous book of interviews, *La philosophie comme manière de vivre*, Paris, LGF, 2003.

and asked how the Ancients dealt with it. The *Treatises* we are reading thus have their origins in the lessons, and are forms of transcription dictated by Plotinus. The Plotinian school was much more a worldly circle of discussion, and the treatises themselves are an expression of this: disorganized, of varying size, not avoiding repetition, they reflect the lively nature of the discussions rather than a closed system. Porphyry himself acknowledges that the early treatises are weaker than the later ones: "[...] the first twenty-one have a less assertive quality and have not yet attained sufficient breadth in terms of the vigor of thought[8]".

Because of the unstructured, non-scholastic nature of the courses, his listeners included a wide variety of profiles: Christians, Gnostic Christians, Sethians (a Gnostic current inspired by the third son of Adam and Eve, Seth), etc. This diversity calls for three immediate clarifications. This diversity calls for three immediate clarifications.

---

8. Porphyry, *Life of Plotinus*, 6, 31-32, *op. cit.*, p. 286.

The first concerns the question of Christianity, and requires us to remember that, at the time, *Christian dogmas were by no means fixed.* The Council of Nicaea, which was to determine the precise objects of the Christian faith, did not take place until 325; so, at the time Plotinus was teaching, something as fundamental to faith as the *creed* was not in force, and Christianity was therefore thought of as a sect, more or less philosophical, whose content was less doctrinal than ethical; in other words, *it was less a question of having faith in this or that than of meditating on the exemplary dimension of Jesus' life.* In short, the years 250-270 were a far cry from the Councils of Nicaea and Constantinople in 381, which would rule on the Holy Spirit and his consubstantiality with the Father. And even further still from the Council of Chalcedon in 451, which laid down the dual nature of Christ, which was not without its troubles. The second clarification concerns the notion of "gnosis", a fundamental concept of Antiquity, and a major issue in both philosophy and theology. Derived from the Greek *gnôsis*, meaning "knowledge", gnosis has two facets, a universal one that determines its fundamentals, and a more specific one that designates a current contemporary with Plotinus. The universal principles of gnosis[9], whatever its period, can be stated as follows: 1) Gnosis is first and foremost a feeling by which *man feels alienated from the world*; the world is not *his* world, he does not feel at home in it and, in this respect, a text such as Plato's *Phaedrus*, where the myth evokes the loss of the soul's wings to account for the human condition[10], perfectly expresses the Gnostic feeling of being fallen and of finding oneself in a world towards which one nourishes a feeling of strangeness. Even the earliest Christians[11], who had no fixed dogmas to adhere to, did not hesitate to associate the Gospels with a certain gnosis. This is the case in chapters 15 and 17 of John's Gospel, where the statement that the

---

9. On this subject, see the excellent collective volume edited by Nathalie Depraz and Jean-François Marquet, *La gnose, une question philosophique*, Paris, Cerf, 2000.

10. Cf. Plato, Phaedo, 246b-c.

11. An author as complex as Clement of Alexandria (150-215), for example, cannot be placed outside gnosis in the general sense of the term: the *Stromata* develop "true gnosis", and celebrate Plato's approach to the ultimate Truth.

disciples are indeed "in the world", but not "of the world[12]", is repeated many times.

2) Gnosis *is gnôsis*, i.e. knowledge, in the sense that it seems to provide salvation. This implies that salvation is not so much linked to death as to knowledge of the profound nature of the real—*reality*—and therefore that *soteriology is correlated with noetics*, in other words that the science of salvation is first and foremost a science of what there is to know. What's more, this implies that salvation can *take place here and now*, in the sense that there's no question of waiting for death in order to know what saves, and that *the conditions of salvation are immanent in that they are buried deep within our being.* As a result, *gnosis attributes a considerable role to the Intellect, since knowledge in the strongest sense of the term is the very operator of salvation*, and salvation can be obtained through a noetic approach that discovers

---

12. Simone Pétrement's now-classic Le Dieu caché (The Hidden God) insists at length that the fourth Gospel—the one generally attributed to John, and which the author attributes to Apollos—is the possible, if not explicit, foundation of Gnostic thought. Cf. Simone Pétrement, Le Dieu séparé. Les origines du gnosticisme, Paris, Cerf, 1984, especially chap. 5 of the second part.

the necessary soteriological elements within oneself. In both these senses, Platonism and Neoplatonism are Gnostic thoughts[13]. But it's important *not to confuse gnosis with gnosticism*[14]. Gnosticism is a trend that emerged in the first and second centuries of the Roman Empire[15], and was certainly derived from Gnosticism,

---

13. Henri-Charles Puech (1902-1986), a leading gnostic scholar, seems to have perfectly captured the gnostic scope of Plotinian thought through inner conversion and immanent discovery of the conditions of salvation: "This interiority is of capital importance for Plotinus' thought : it enables him to develop a *mysticism of immanence* within the framework of a *metaphysics of transcendence*", Henri-Charles Puech, "Position spirituelle et signification de Plotin", [1938], *in* Henri-Charles Puech, *En quête de la gnose*, tome I, *La gnose et le temps*, Paris, Gallimard, 1978, p.. 69.

14. In this, we follow Antoine Faivre's—in our view unquestionable— indications in *Accès de l'ésotérisme occidental*, tome I, Paris, Gallimard, 1996, particularly the chapter entitled "Sources antiques et médiévales des courants ésotériques modernes".

15. Regarding the philosophical aspect of Gnosticism, we can only refer to the studies of Hans Jonas, notably *La religion gnostique. Le message du Dieu étranger et les débuts du christianisme*, translation Louis Evrard, Paris, Flammarion, 1978, as well as the short introduction to *La gnose et l'esprit de l'Antiquité tardive*, translation Nathalie Frogneux, Mimésis, 2019. We can also refer to Éric Voegelin's work on the political significance of gnosis, in particular *Sciences, politique et gnose*, Paris, Bayard, 2004.

but it was a very specific trend that we know only in the indirect form of the refutations it received. No doubt conceived as a reaction to the relatively recent—and particularly strange—concept of creation, Gnosticism sought less to reject the notion of creation than to make it compatible with a sense of worldly decay. To understand what was at stake in this trend, we need to remember that the notion of creation, taken in its radical sense of creation *ex nihilo*—from nothing—was totally foreign to the Greeks and Romans alike, who could not conceive of the possibility of moving from nothing to being. Of all the notions that would form the core of Christian dogma, that of creation *ex nihilo* was undoubtedly the most disconcerting in terms of reason in general, but also in terms of the reception it received at the time. This is why Gnosticism seems to be a Gnostic response to the emergence of the idea that the world was created by a transcendent power, and not simply *configured* or *ordered* by an Architect. Indeed, given the obvious suffering implied by the world's material dimension, it seems extremely difficult to consider that a just—if not good—God would himself be the creator of such a situation. This leads to an alternative: either we renounce this destabilizing concept of creation, or we maintain it, but then we cannot judge that a just God is the author of the material world. The second option lies at the heart of Gnosticism, which obviously stems from a sense of the world's strangeness, and therefore correlates it with the need for an unjust or evil God to have created the material world. According to this perspective, the material body is demonized, conceived as the work of the Evil One, the Demiurge, or even Yahweh assimilated to the Evil One (Marcion's version), while the spirit is that which relates us to the good God, who manifests himself to man through the spirit. The central figures are Simon the Magus (d. 65), Valentinus (d. 160), Marcion (85-160) and Basilides (d. 140), each of whom gave rise to their own particular strand of Gnosticism.

We must therefore bear in mind a subtlety linked to this context: *when Plotinus condemns gnosis, we must always understand gnosticism* as a dualism hostile to matter, and not gnosis as such, which is a

feeling of strangeness towards the world and a noetic through which salvation comes about; Plotinus is not a dualist, he does not condemn matter, but he makes the conversion of the soul to Intellect the very condition of a certain salvation, but also of a certain ethic; in our eyes, therefore, *Plotinus embodies the archetype of the gnostic philosopher refusing gnosticism. On the other hand, gnosis is a universal metaphysics and sentiment that clearly predates Christianity*, and can be found far beyond Christian thinkers.

The third point concerns the Church's relationship with gnosis. Many Christians are tempted by gnosis in general, and even by gnosticism in particular, notably Marcionism, which establishes an unbridgeable distance between the Old and New Testaments. Nevertheless, a number of theologians wrote and condemned Gnosis as much as Gnosticism, starting with Irenaeus of Lyons (130-202), whose famous treatise *Against Heresies. Dénonciation et réfutation de la gnose au nom menteur (Denunciation and refutation of gnosis with a lying name)*, written around 180 and turned against Simon the Magus and Valentinus, was a great success. It's worth recalling what a heresy is, in the literal sense of the term: it comes from the Greek *hairêsis*, meaning "school of thought", or "choice of thought". Basically, a heresy is first and foremost a *bias* in favor of a particular thought, and any philosophical school is called *hairêsis* in Greek. So the notion of *hairêsis* is initially a choice or a particular orientation; but, with the help of Christian theology, this notion will undergo two inflections: 1) in relation to the universal Church, it will appear as seditious because particularistic, whereas the Church calls itself "Catholic", i.e. literally "universal", which excludes particular orientations, and 2) in relation to dogma, it will appear as false. A heresy will thus gradually lose its original Greek meaning and become an attack on the unity of a dogma held by the universal Church. But not only does this mean that a thought is heretical only in relation to a dogma and never in itself, it also only makes sense when dogmas are fixed, thus creating a retrospective optical effect. Consequently, in Plotinus' day, it was impossible to distinguish between a Gnostic and a

Christian, and when Plotinus wrote his treatise against the Gnostics (*Ennead* II, 9, Treatise 33), it was a treatise against Gnosticism that, in part, also concerned certain Christians; It should not be forgotten that Porphyry would later write a *treatise against Christians*, and it's not certain that for thinkers like Plotinus or Porphyry[16] the difference between "gnostics" and "Christians" was clear-cut.

Much later, the Council of Nicaea (325) condemned Gnosticism, although Marcionism—which involved the status of the Old Testament texts[17]—was condemned as early as 144.

The end of Plotinus' life was very sad; in 268, he had to separate from Porphyry, who was melancholy

---

16. Cf. Porphyry's ambiguities in the *Letter to Marcella*, translation by Arnaud Perrot, Paris, Les Belles Lettres, 2019.

17. Fortunately, we have a translation of a major book by theologian Adolf von Harnack (1851-1930), a specialist in the history of Christian dogma, and therefore of Gnosticism: Adolf von Harnack, *Marcion. L'Évangile du Dieu étranger*, collective translation, Paris, Cerf, 2004.

and developing suicidal tendencies; Porphyry thus left Rome for Lilybaea in Sicily, in the hope of finding rest and peace there. In the same year, Gallien was assassinated, so that the protection afforded by the Emperor's wife, Salonina, no longer held. Plotinus had to leave Rome. A year later, in 269, Amelius—his first disciple—left him to join the Neoplatonist school of Numenius of Apamea, often referred to as Numenius, of whom some twenty fragments have been found. Thus, lonely, ill and exhausted, Plotinus went to Campania, the Italian region where Naples is located, and died there in 270, perhaps of tuberculosis.

The Soul Soaring "out there" or the Exemplarity of a Life

Porphyry—as we have amply demonstrated—is interested in Plotinus' life in order to make it exemplary and thus to construct an ethical model, but such an approach is the *result of* a certain approach to the world, not a *decision*; in other words, what remains to be clarified are the profound reasons why the description of a man's life is not the same as that of an individuality.

One of the hardest things for us to grasp, given our mental distance from ancient—and medieval—thought, is that we take it for granted that my relationship with myself should be to myself, *independently of the rest of the world*. Indeed, we tend to take it for granted that the relationship with oneself is one of delimitation and, consequently, isolation. For a Greek thinker, however, this false contemporary self-evidence is the exact opposite: to relate to myself is to discover my place within a whole infinitely greater than my particularity, which, as its name suggests, is precisely *part of* a whole. In this respect, we understand what the Greeks call the "soul" (*psyche*), that animating principle that is both me and more than me, which is to say that the "me" cannot have the meaning it has today.

In Greek, *psyche* is first and foremost a *principle* that can be distributed according to both life and thought. In other words, the *psyche* is a principle of life and/or a principle of thought, with "principle" to be understood in the sense of a first cause, a causal origin of a given phenomenon. In this respect, the *psyche* is in no way defined by the notion of personality or individuality. The Latin *anima* perhaps expresses in a more familiar way the role of this principle, which is that of *animation*: the soul is thus a principle of life in that it *animates* body and thought. From this we can immediately deduce that thought is *movement*, and that the object of thought will itself be moved by the soul; we need to understand in what sense this motion of cognitive objects can be understood.

The science of this soul as animating principle is called *psychology*, which is in no way to be confused with psychology in the contemporary sense, which, reduced to a human science, confines itself to studying the emotional and empirical states of the subject. On the contrary, psychology in the ancient sense—in the authentic sense, we should say—aims to account for the *vital breath* animating all things, although the very term *psychology* was only coined belatedly by the Croatian Marko Marulic (1450-1524) in his treatise *Psichiologia de ratione animae humanae*.

It follows from the preceding remarks that *the soul cannot be reserved for man*, who possesses neither the exclusivity of life nor that of thought; every animate thing possesses a soul as the principle of this animation: living beings, plants, beasts, men, moving stars, gods, the world in its entirety, these are all entities whose movement can only be conceived by the presence of a driving soul, which is indeed a *principle* and not *an individuality*.

For Plato, this idea is reinforced by the fact that the world itself has a soul, ensuring its movement and unity. As the world is not immobile or devoid of activity, it must be animated by a *principle*, and this animating principle naturally takes the name of soul. The soul of the world (*tou pantos psyché*) was a constant theme in philosophy, even for Schelling, who in 1798 evoked a *Weltseele* in a work with the evocative title *De l'âme du monde (On the Soul of the World)*.

We still need to clarify the relationship between the soul and the human being, and whether the soul is the explanatory or causal principle of what we are. Certainly, from a Platonic perspective, the soul and man are extremely close; it is what animates man both bodily and noetically, so much so that it is permissible to propose an equivalence between man in his human nature and the soul itself. In this respect, *Alcibiades* attempts to justify such an equivalence in the following terms:

"Therefore, since neither the body nor the whole is man, I believe it remains that man is nothing or, if he is something, it must be recognized that it can be nothing other than the soul[18]."

We can therefore say with Socrates that "the soul is man[19]" and immediately deduce that the improvement of the soul is nothing other than the question of the improvement of man. But then, let's ask the question again: what does it mean to improve the soul, i.e. to

---

18. Plato, *Alcibiades*, 130c, translation by Chantal Marbœuf and Jean-François Pradeau, Paris, GF, 2000, p. 173.
19. *Ibid.*

improve man? The *Phaedo* may offer the beginnings of an answer. In a close discussion with Cebes, Socrates describes two types of soul activity. The first, linked to its motor function in the body, leads it to the latter, which it uses for all sensations. In this case, the soul "is dragged by the body in the direction of that which never even remains but itself, and here it is prey to wandering, confusion, vertigo, as if it were drunk, all because it is with this kind of thing that it is in contact[20]." For Plato, to feel is to bring the soul to the body; to experience a sensation is to let the hindered soul merge with the body in order to feel the impressions affecting the latter. As bodies are interdependent with one another, the soul is carried along by this multiplicity, these encounters, these shocks that it feels, and which reveal the nature of bodies. Lacking identity and stability, and subject to time, material bodies carry the soul into the dizzy world of ephemerality and instability, condemning it to wander among the corruptible. The result is a chain of desires never satiated by the law of perpetual novelty,

---

20. Plato, *Phœdon*, 79c, translation by Monique Dixsaut, Paris, GF, 1991, p. 242

worldly dispersion and the inability to find unity. To alienate oneself from the world of bodies is, for the soul, to condemn oneself to finding neither rest nor unity. In other words, in the world of material bodies governed by time, change, difference and corruption reign, and the soul, amalgamated with the body in order to feel, feels dizzy as it is caught up in the structural impermanence of the material world.

However, the soul is not only driven to turn towards bodies, to feel. It can also soar "out there, towards that which is pure and everlasting, which is immortal and ever self-similar[21]." The soul can soar towards the eternal, towards that which escapes the corruption of time, towards that which is identical to itself and not corrupted by difference. This notion of "out there" [*ékei*], crucial in Plotinus' work, designates the set of intelligible realities—immutable, absolute and eternal realities—towards which the soul can therefore direct itself. To put it another way, intelligible realities are the

---

21. *Ibid,* 79d, p. 242.

very structure of the real—reality—and this structure is accessible only to the intellect, towards which the soul, in its rational part, can lead us. Hence, if the soul discards or turns away from the body, it turns towards itself to relate to intelligible realities. And Plato concludes:

"In its proximity to these beings, it always remains the same as itself, since it is in contact with them. This state of the soul is what we call thought [*phronesis*][22]."

At last, we can answer our opening question. As a principle of animation, the soul can become sensation or thought. In the first case, it turns away from itself, ceases to reflect, and alienates itself from the bodies it encounters: staggering, wandering, it sails at the mercy of the impermanence of the material world. But at the same time, this sensation signals a kind of self-fettering on the part of the soul. On the other hand, *concentrated* within itself, it draws closer to that which is identical to itself, to eternal movement, to that which never changes

---

22. *Ibid.*

and which time never corrupts. The soul's improvement can therefore have only one meaning: that of a progressive apprenticeship in the soul's relationship to itself, of the soul's investigation of itself with a view to tearing itself away from the corruptible precariousness of the world to coil itself in the identity and eternity of the movement of being.

Nevertheless, we can no longer conceal the incomplete nature of such an answer. Why would the soul's *concentration* on itself bring it into contact with eternal realities? Furthermore, in the case of infrahuman beings such as plants or even animals, is it the same soul that is capable of concentrating on itself and thus reaching "out there" among intelligible realities? On the one hand, this raises the question of the soul's relationship to the intelligible, and on the other, the universality of this relationship: is every soul capable of the intelligible?

Let's start by answering the second question. Every body, be it plant, animal or human, has a certain

number of needs necessary for its survival; such needs can monopolize the entire activity of the soul, which in this situation can in no way exercise its intellective function. In other words, for plants and animals, the soul is of the same nature as for men or gods, but the bodily constitution that impedes it clearly prevents it from exercising its highest function. For this reason, and for plants and animals, it is limited to ensuring the preservation of life.

But if the soul is indeed the same by nature, differing only in the functions it performs in the bodies it animates, how can we determine its proper nature? Is it itself corporeal, which would explain why it can animate bodies? Is it intelligible, which would explain why it can move thought? Or is it a kind of intermediary between sensible bodies and intelligible realities? Plato's answer, in both the *Phaedo* and the *Timaeus*, is unequivocal: *the soul is an intermediary reality* that is not at all material, yet at the same time not fully intelligible. It maintains a kind of asymmetrical relationship with intelligible realities, to which it desires to be ever more like, but *such a desire for resemblance paradoxically indicates a difference, not an identity*. The soul can only desire to resemble intelligible realities if it differs from them, despite all its efforts to get closer. Moreover, this resemblance is of the order of desire rather than of accomplishment: while it does indeed come closer to intelligible forms, the latter cannot resemble the soul, so that it is preferable to speak of a *desire* for resemblance rather than of an accomplished resemblance, since intelligible realities in no way resemble the soul. The difference that remains between the soul and intelligible realities indicates that the soul is different to itself: far from always being identical to itself, it evolves over time, and faculties appear and disappear within it.

The nature of the soul is therefore highly paradoxical and difficult to define. On the one hand, as Socrates states in the *Phaedrus*, "every soul is immortal[23]", an immortality demonstrated by the fact that the soul

---

23. Plato, *Phaedrus*, 245c, translation by Luc Brisson, Paris, GF, 2000, p. 116.

moves itself, in the knowledge that a self-moving being can neither be annihilated nor come to be. As such, the soul has something divine about it, since the first property of the divine is immortality. "Once we have demonstrated the immortality of that which moves itself, we will not be ashamed to assert that this is where the soul's being resides, and that this is indeed what its definition consists of[24]." But *this immortality does not lead to immutability*: the soul can neither be destroyed nor begotten, but on the other hand it is fulfilled in duration, so that it can both *approach* the stable eternity of the intelligible and at the same time be *attached* to the sensible, which drags it along with it in change, rendering resemblance ineffective.

Let the soul concentrate on itself, then, and it will be able, by virtue of its very nature, to relate to the eternal; on the other hand, it will only be able to indicate to those who use their soul reflexively a certain approach to the intelligible, failing to provide it with a

---

24. *Ibid*, 245e, p. 117.

perfect identity. In other words, *the soul's relationship with the intelligible remains a distant one, the distance being constituted by* dianoia, *i.e. by rational thought itself.* Reasoning or thought in its content is both what gives us access to the structure of reality—intelligible reality—and at the same time what keeps us distant from it—separating us from intelligible reality the rational deployment of thought, which constitutes a kind of intermediary between soul and reality. This aspect will be decisive in understanding what Plotinus calls the *Logoi.*

But once we have clarified the nature of the soul, we can at the same time resolve the question of the relationship between it and man: both are intermediate realities oscillating between the materiality of the body and the elevation of thought, between sensible needs and the grasp of intelligible realities. While not every soul is a man, it is necessary to understand that the soul is the very nature of man, insofar as it expresses this intermediary nature that is so difficult to situate. In this respect, it is possible to say that what makes this man this man is his soul, as Plato affirms in the

Alcibiades[25]. But we still need to clarify one point, and understand exactly what we're saying when we assert that the *psyche* is Socrates or so-and-so. Jean-Pierre Vernant seems to us to have formulated this ambiguity with great clarity:

"The *psukhé* [*psyche*] is Socrates, but not Socrates' "I" […]. The *psukhe* is in each of us an impersonal or suprapersonal entity. It is *the* soul in me rather than *my* soul[26]."

The soul, as we've said, is the principle of movement and, as such, performs this function in all things; furthermore, it is not born with me, nor does it die with me, and so it does *not belong to* me, which is why Vernant can say that it is not *my* soul in the sense that it is *only* mine. So, while there is a plurality of souls that make things what they are, the fact remains that

---

25. Cf. Plato, *Alcibiades*, 130c.
26. Jean-Pierre Vernant, *L'individu, la mort, l'amour. Soi-même et l'autre en Grèce ancienne*, Paris, Gallimard, coll. Folio histoire, 1989, p. 227-228.

all these souls—eternal and therefore divine—exert a force through which we can rediscover the divine. In man, it is by exerting its rational part that the soul can rediscover the intelligible and, consequently, rediscover the very structuring of reality. As *a* result, *the soul is not complacent about its own singularity but, on the contrary, strives to rediscover universality—i.e., the intelligible.* Vernant continues: "The immortal soul is not the expression of man's singular psychology, but rather the aspiration of the individual subject to melt into the whole, to reintegrate himself into the general cosmic order[27]."

This is how Plotinus' biographical question comes to be understood: the description of his life only makes sense if it describes the soul that inhabits it and enables him to rise—movement—towards the structuring of reality, towards the intelligible, and thus to leave himself behind by renouncing the illusions of singularity. To put it another way, an exemplary life

---

27. *Ibid*, p. 228.

is *exemplary* only insofar as it is able to indicate the means to avoid indulging in individuality, while at the same time making the soul the principle by which not *my* personality but, on the contrary, the universal sense of being can be found within oneself.

Enneads Edition

Thirty years after Plotinus' death, Porphyry, who had collected the texts dictated by the latter, published the *Enneads* between 300 and 301, to which he added a short biography of Plotinus as an introduction.

Porphyry not only compiles the latter's works, but also sorts them, dividing or merging them to classify them in a particular order that can be described as logico-thematic, while attributing to them titles that will have an impact on the interpretation of certain concepts—starting with that of hypostasis.

This creates two different series of Plotinus' works. The first is chronological in nature, and refers to the temporal order in which the Treatises were written, i.e. the order in which Plotinus dictated them. But what we literally call the *Enneads,* which means "nine" in Greek, is a construction by Porphyry that groups blocks of nine treatises thematically into six Enneads. In short, *each Ennead contains nine treatises in an order that has been liberated from that of the writing and replaced by that of thematic unity.* This creates a permanent double referencing that we must learn to decipher.

The six Enneads are distributed as follows:

-The first concerns ethics, i.e. a certain way of behaving, thinking and considering the world—in short, *a certain way of inhabiting the world and, more importantly, of learning to use the world as a basis for tracing its fundamental structure.*

-The second and third Enneads are devoted to nature, whose meaning in Plotinus engages a whole reflection on the soul, the Intellect, and the "reasons" that we will define in the course of the work.

-The fourth ennead is devoted to the soul.

-The fifth is dedicated to Intellect.

-The sixth is dedicated to the One.

As for the Treaties, it is estimated that the order of drafting is roughly as follows:

-From 254 to 263, the first twenty-one were dictated and written, and Porphyry tells us that they were probably of lesser quality than those that followed.

-From 263 to 268, treatises 22 to 45 were dictated and written.

-In 269, in the midst of the turmoil, treatises 46 to 50 were dictated and drafted.

-In 270, on the threshold of his life, Plotinus is said to have dictated treatises 51 to 54.

There are several editions of the Enneads, but the most significant is undoubtedly that of Marsilio Ficino (1433-1499), a leading figure in Florentine Neoplatonism who, after translating Plato from Greek into Latin, completed the same task for Plotinus in 1486. This translation was not published until 1492 in Florence, however, and it is still customary to refer to it to clarify certain philological choices. Nevertheless, the two reference editions today are those of Paul Henry and Hans-Rudolf Schwyzer, who have proposed two versions of the *Plotini Opera*, a so-called major version published between 1951 and 1973[28], containing a remarkable critical apparatus, and a so-called minor version, with fewer notes and amended text, published between 1964 and 1982.[29]

There is no particular key for establishing the correspondence between Treatises and Enneads; on the other hand, the Treatise number gives an indication of the date of writing, while the classification within the Ennead provides thematic information; if we take Treatise 30, for example, we know that it was written between 263 and 268, and if we take its equivalent in Ennead, it is Ennead III, 8, which means that it is the eighth treatise of the third Ennead, and therefore concerns nature.

Thus, the reference "Plotinus, *Ennead* V, 2 [11], 1, 27-29" should be read as follows: this is the second

---

28. Cf. Paul Henry and Hans-Rudolf Schwyzer (eds.), *Plotini Opera*, three volumes, Paris/Brussels, Desclée de Brouwer/Édition universelle, 1951-1973.

29. Cf. Paul Henry and Hans-Rudolf Schwyzer (eds.), *Plotini Opera*, three volumes, Oxford, Oxford Classical Texts, 1964-1982.

treatise of the fifth Ennead, corresponding to Treatise 11, first chapter, lines 27-29. But the reference can also be written "Plotinus, Treatise 11 (V, 2), 1, 27-29", in which case it refers to the first Treatise 11, corresponding to the second treatise of the fifth Ennead, chapter 1, lines 27 to 29.

Finally, while we'll be using the translation of the Treatises edited by Luc Brisson and Jean-François Pradeau (GF[30]), we also recommend the isolated editions of certain treatises published by LGF, in particular Treatises 9, 25, 38, 50 and 51, whose commentary is commendable.

---

30. Cf. Plotinus, *Treatises*, published in eight volumes by Garnier-Flammarion from 2002 to 2010, edited by Luc Brisson and Jean-François Pradeau. As is customary, in the notes we mention the Ennead number, the treatise number, the chapter, the lines, all followed by the pagination in the GF edition.

Chapter I: From Nature [Phusis] to the Soul

We begin with this notion, because it seems to us to constitute the pivot of the whole of Plotinian thought, the one around which the first three and last three Enneads are organized in mirror image. Because it involves matter and bodies, as well as soul and Intellect, it must be described, defined and analyzed from the outset, in order to introduce all the decisive notions that Plotinus can develop.

1) General Information

Physis in Greek comes from the verb *phuo*, meaning "I make grow", "I give birth", and from *phuomaï*, "I grow", "I believe", "I am born". The Greeks always thought of nature as an autonomous power, a power of growth, birth and the organization of life in its broadest sense, i.e. in the sense of that which is "animated", i.e. that which has a soul (*psyche*). In this respect, the gods are part of nature, and it would be hard to find in the Greeks what we have come to call "supernatural": strictly speaking, nothing is truly supernatural for the Greeks, for whom nature has a far greater and more encompassing extension than it does for us.

The immediate consequence of this approach is that *nature is not so much a thing, or even a set of fixed things, as a process and a dynamic*; nature is an activity of outpouring, of production, and cannot be identified with fixed entities. In this respect, we must avoid turning nature into a kind of object designation, but rather understand it as a force of constant production—which helps us to understand the intrinsic link between nature and the animation of the soul.

Finally, *phusis* has a normative dimension: it is the law that regulates phenomena, and is often also the soul that enlivens bodies.

Beyond these three general characteristics of *phusis*, we must add the Stoic vision of phusis, without which Plotinian thought would remain unintelligible. For the Stoics, with whom Plotinus was well acquainted, nature is both the whole and the absolute, which is to say that we find ourselves in a monistic ontology in which nothing can be truly *external* to nature. Nature even governs the whole through natural, rational, necessary and perfect laws. Nature is therefore divine. Add to this the fact that, for the Stoics, nature is also *my* nature. This shift is easily explained on two grounds: 1) firstly, because I am brought to be incorporated into the whole, so that I undergo a natural legality that incorporates me into the whole. And 2) because I have received the *logos*, the reason, which is constitutive of my nature and which "wills" order, i.e. the submission of the parts to the whole. In this respect, the ideal is to ensure that *our* nature lives according to nature, which can be summed up in these three ways:

-Nature is the divine whole.

-Nature is my nature.

-Since my nature is to possess *logos*, then nature is a form of psychic rationality, a rational soul immanent in the world, a thesis that Plotinus will discuss at length.

2) Plotinian Meaning of Nature: The Challenge of the Logoi

a) The notion of logoï

To understand Plotinus' approach to nature, we need to keep in mind the generalities mentioned above, and at the same time introduce the complex issue of *logos*, the plural of *logos* whose translation is a matter of some debate. The great difficulty inherent in this term is that it seems to refer to a faculty—reason—, to a linguistic development—speech or discourse—, to the very development of reason—reasoning—or even to knowledge. In fact, what all these approaches have in common seems to be that of *development*: *logos* seems to develop or unfold articulated things over time, whether it's an ordered thought, i.e. reasoning, discourse or even knowledge. Let's say, then, that *logos always expresses an ordered development according to rules*, and that *nothing is more misleading than to identify* logos with *my* reason. But, by the very fact that we develop something—thought, discourse, reasoning—we find ourselves caught up in a duration, in a certain time that conditions development. As a result, *logos* appears as the development or explicitation of a fundamental reality, itself presupposing a certain milieu—time or duration—through which development is possible.

This question of development involving time is absolutely crucial, for Plotinus, however syncretic his thinking, retains a series of Platonic notions, starting with that of "Form", *eidos*. Now, it's commonplace to point out that Form, as the absolute, unchanging reality of things, escapes time. For this reason, Form as an eternal and unchanging reality cannot, as such, be given in time, and it is extremely difficult to think of the possibility that forms could be the structure of otherwise temporal realities: how could that which is perfectly foreign to time inform—structure—in any way whatsoever a series of temporally determined bodies? The only solution, then, is to summon the *logos*, the "reasons", i.e. the rational developments that enable the Forms to unfold, develop and *clarify* themselves. We can thus consider that if *logos* is a development—discourse, speech, reasoning, etc.— it's because it's a development.-This is because it develops or makes explicit something that, by itself, has no scope. Hence, we understand that Form is by itself without development—which is why it can only be known intuitively—and that *logos* "de-develops" or makes it explicit. In short, *logos and* "reasons" are the actual development of Forms which, being non-temporal, cannot in themselves contain any development whatsoever. *Logoi* cannot be conceived without Forms, but Forms can be conceived without Logoi.

The problem that now arises is that of the substrate in which *logos* can develop. Logoi can only develop in matter, which means that in the very heart of matter, reasons unfold an order and structure whose origin is intelligible. This is best illustrated by the example of beauty, which, as such, is a Form, and therefore a

fundamental ontological structure, and which unfolds according to reasons in matter, in order to structure bodies made beautiful in this way. "So then," writes Plotinus, "a beautiful body is beautiful through a community [*koinonaia*] with a reason [*logos*] from the gods[31]."

b) Nature, world and Logoi

Let's take this reasoning a step further and apply it to nature, and *then* to the world. The world is full of particular bodies, especially living bodies. Each body is what it is only insofar as it is the development in matter of reasons which themselves develop forms, which is to say that *bodies and matter are not exactly the same thing: the body is the product of matter informed by reasons*, so that *the body is always ordered by the very fact that it is by nature the bearer of rational order.*

On the other hand, all bodies form the world; but, precisely, how is it that we say *the* world? Why does this collection of bodies form a unified element, the world?

---

31. Plotinus, *Enneads* I, 6, [1], 2, 30, p. 70.

First of all, this indicates that the world is eternal and incorruptible, that it remains identical to itself, and that it therefore constitutes a kind of perfect body, unlike individual, perishable and corruptible bodies. But such perfection can only be understood through a principle of unity that makes all bodies appear to be a kind of partition of the perfect body that is the world. This explains why the sum of all bodies does not form a gigantic chaos: quite simply, individual bodies are *second*, not *first*; they are already the partition of the world as a unity[32], which requires us to think in terms of the principle of unity, and thus to posit a soul of the world, the notion of which we encountered in the introduction through its Platonic usage.

---

32. Treatise 31 posits both the unity of the world and the *rational method for representing it*: "This world, then, let us grasp by discursive thought, in each of its parts [...], taking them all together to unify them as far as possible, so that, as soon as one appears [...] then we immediately picture the sun, and with it the stars, and we see the Earth, the sea and all living things, as in a transparent sphere through which it would really be possible to see everything. "Plotinus, *Ennead* V, 8 [31], 9, 1-7, p. 103.

However, *the soul of the world is not yet nature*, if only because of the definition of nature we have just recalled, which points to a process of production, whereas the soul is rather a principle of animation and, where applicable, of movement towards the intelligible. Nevertheless, although nature and the soul of the world are not identical, it is not possible to think of them separately. For this reason, we can say that nature in its Plotinian sense *is* first and foremost nature, and therefore an expression of unity, and it is for this reason that *nature presupposes the soul of the world*. To put it another way, *the soul of the world provides nature with its unity, justifying our speaking of nature*. In short, nature is that which is ordered by the soul of the world and which, as a force of production, *therefore produces in an orderly fashion*. What does this mean in concrete terms? Quite simply, the process of production that *is* nature consists in developing reasons in matter, and thus producing bodies that will be expressions of the world. In short, nature is the dynamic process by which matter is informed in the form of bodies referring to the unity of the world, i.e. the formation of beings materially developing Forms—bodies—all belonging to the world whose unity is ensured by the soul, which relates to the world only through nature. In other words, *nature is the means by which the soul of the world actually has a world.*

This has several consequences. The first concerns individual bodies, i.e. matter informed by reasons. Just as the real is not reality, so the body is not corporeality: if the body is the result of information, there must be a nature of bodies by which matter must be informed. In other words, *corporality is made up of reasons*, which in turn refer to Forms. As a result, corporeity is a Form that is fulfilled only by reasons encountering matter[33], while body designates matter informed by reasons.

The second consequence has to do with the reasons themselves: if we judge that corporeity is in itself a Form that is fulfilled only by reasons, then there are necessarily two types of *logoi*: the first type refers to

---

33. Cf. Plotinus, II, 7, [37], 3, 3-16, p. 390.

what we might call pure *logoi* that are necessitated by corporeity as a Form, and the second are the *logoi* actually developed in time and through which bodies come into being. To put it another way, in their purity, the *Logoi* must be properties of the Intellect, but in their development they must be movements in matter animated by a soul. Naturally, we've mainly been talking about developed *Logoi*, explaining the Forms, although the very analysis of their existence presupposes the admission of reasons from the Intellect, without which the very possibility that the Forms could develop rationally would become unintelligible.

But, despite appearances, we're still not quite out of the woods when it comes to the complexity of what Plotinus calls "nature"; to fully understand this formative process, we need to dig even deeper into its conceptuality, and take a close look at Treatise 5 (*Ennead* V, 9), particularly chapter 6.

c) Logoï spermatikoï

In the introductory generalities, we mentioned the Stoic approach to nature as an essential element in understanding Plotinian conceptuality, but so far we have made little use of this reference, a situation that needs to be remedied.

Plotinian thought, it should be remembered, is a complex synthesis of Platonism, Aristotelianism and Stoicism, the latter developing a series of concepts around the *logos spermatikon* or *logoi spermatikoi*. A materialistic, monistic system, Stoicism arrives at the idea that nothing is foreign to the matter of the world governed by nature. There is therefore a general, indeterminate matter, which nonetheless adopts several differentiated forms according to the rational ordering of nature. So where does the possibility for each particular body to take the form it does come from? The Stoic answer lies in the concept of *logoi spermatikoi*, or generating principles immanent to matter. These are corporeal entities that contain the form and laws of growth of each individual body, which can be deduced from Stoicism's radically monistic ontology, for which the order of development of things can only be immanent to the world itself. These generative principles, immanent to the matter of the world, explain not only the formation of individual bodies, whether living or inert, but also their development.

Plotinus takes up this notion of *logoi spermatikoi* with the notion of "seeds" developed in Treatise 37, except that, as a good Platonist, he cannot be monistic in the Stoic sense. They are within it, and therefore not material, not "corporeal". In this way, Plotinus can clarify the meaning of a material body beyond what we've already said: the body is a soul which, having a *logos spermatikon*, a "seed", is able to sow formless matter to give it the precise shape of a body and impose the laws of its development. This seed is not material, and therefore contains no parts, which is why in the seed the parts are not distinct, since distinction presupposes a sharing that only extended matter makes possible.

Yet the fact is that the eye differs from the hand, and so there must be a reason for the eye and a reason for the hand, although these reasons, not being material, cannot in the seed be thought of as distinctions. Basically, Plotinus understands very well that when we think of a difference, we tend to spatialize it, to extend it and to conceive of it as a *division*; but for immaterial realities—and such is the case of seeds—this makes no sense, so that we cannot assert that they are distinct.

Nevertheless, if we continue to examine chapter 6, particularly lines 19 and 20, we realize that Plotinus draws a distinction between two souls, since on the one hand, the seeds are in the soul, while on the other, the soul is in the seeds. The former is the soul of each thing, the soul of each individuality, and the soul of each individuality contains the seeds, i.e. the *logoi spermatikoi*, by which bodies will be individually informed, individually sown; but let's not forget that bodies are like partitions of the world, which presupposes a world soul, a general soul of the *cosmos*, taken as a perfect and incorruptible whole, and of which all bodies, informed by the *logoi*, are the unified expression. This is precisely what the Stoics call "nature". In this respect, it's easy to understand what Plotinus takes from the Stoics, and at the same time what he denies them. He borrows this from them, namely that nature is indeed, if we go back to its source, a form of psychic rationality, i.e. rationality associated with a soul, i.e. a rational soul. Nature is simply the unity of bodies via a rational soul that runs through the very matter of the world. But at the same time, because of his Platonism, Plotinus rejects Stoic monism; as a result, the soul cannot be of the same nature as bodies, which explains why Plotinus distinguishes between the rational soul and nature itself, unlike the Stoics, for whom nature is the rational soul that governs the world. For Plotinus, *phusis* deploys reasons from an element foreign to bodies, namely from the soul of the world, so that the latter can no longer be that into which nature spreads in immanent form.

Two essential points follow from this: 1) since nature presupposes a psychic principle of unity, i.e. a soul, it becomes possible to link nature to contemplation; the delicate Treatise 30 can only be understood in this way; 2) in Plotinus, material bodies always refer to "another", to "out there", to something that is not

immanent to the world, and that is ontologically differentiated; historically speaking, Plotinus does not take
up Stoic monism, so the world refers to something other
than itself. In other words, the world and nature are not
the same thing: the world is the unity of the bodies that
make up its partition, while nature refers to the soul of
the world present in each seed, a seed that enables the
body to be said to be *natural*.

d) How can nature contemplate?

This question is at the heart of Treatise 30, which
may seem confusing, but chapter 1 fully assumes
the problem. Acknowledging that nature as such
is devoid of reflection and *phronesis*, which can be
deduced from the very fact that it is only ever the lower
part of the soul of the world, Plotinus returns to the
Stoic view that nature cannot reflect. But, unlike the
latter, Plotinus introduces a Platonic concept, that of
image, which allows us to think about the fact that
what the soul is capable of, nature is also capable of,
at least as an image, something that Treatise 28 had

already theorized[34]. That nature is productive, but not reflexive, means that, *in relation to the soul,* it can only correspond to its lower, i.e. *vegetative*, part. This is a crucial point, since the vegetative part of the soul is neither reflexive nor thinking, but nevertheless refers to the soul of the world, of which it is the lower part. However, the continuity inherent in Plotinism means that it is *indeed the same soul that can think, reflect, represent itself and have a vegetative lower part.* In other words, there must be a link of continuity between the lower, vegetative part and the upper, thinking and reflecting part, which is to say that *the productive part that produces bodies through the diffusion of reasons is linked to reflection and therefore contemplation*—and this will be the profound reason for the contemplative scope of nature, provided we think afresh about the extension of such contemplation.

Traditionally, contemplation, or *theôria*, is reserved for man and the gods, and designates the activity through which *the intellect* gains access to reality

---

34. Cf. in particular *Ennead* IV, 4 [38], 13, 2-25, p. 134.

itself, i.e. to intelligibles. As a result, only realities pertaining to the intelligible, to the very structure of reality, are capable of *theôria*. But what we've seen with Plotinus requires us to extend the meaning of *theôria*. Because there are intelligible forms whose temporal development is called "reasons", which inform matter and produce bodies, "nature" being the name of this production process from the soul of the world. But this is tantamount to saying that the intelligible is found *mediately* in bodies, that nature diffuses the intelligible via reasons into bodies, and that *a natural reality is basically a reality materially exemplifying the intelligibles in a temporally developed form*. More than a Platonic reflection, this is a diffusion of the very structure of reality—reality—within reality. In short, there is the intelligible in bodies, and therefore in natural beings. Moreover, nature depends on the soul of the world, a unified soul that, while producing through its vegetative part, becomes thinking and reflexive through its higher part; the soul of the world therefore *knows* what it is doing and does not produce blindly; it knows full well that it diffuses reasons into matter to inform it, and it knows full well that the reasons come from the intelligible. As a result, Plotinus resemantizes the notion of *theôria*: it is no longer solely a theoretical activity of knowing the intelligibles, but also becomes a practical activity, i.e. a productive activity. In other words, *the very fact of the soul's unity* implies the need for natural production not to be at odds with thought and reflection, even though, as such, nature does not think. But since natural production—or nature as a process of production—engages the intelligible, and since the soul is one, then contemplation must be opened up *beyond theoretical activity, i.e. natural production must be brought into the very heart of contemplation.*

Here, almost in retrospect, is the reason why so much time had to be devoted to clarifying concepts in order to distinguish their meaning. For Plotinus, nature is neither matter nor bodies. Matter is the formless starting material; it is a kind of material available to be informed. Bodies are the product of matter informed by reasons or seeds. Nature is the process of diffusion of Form via reasons, whose agent, i.e. active principle, is the soul of the world in its lower, vegetative sense. Consequently, once each of these definitions is understood, it becomes clear that the body as natural body can contemplate, but in a very precise sense: in the sense that *in its* very *naturalness* is played out the unity of the soul of the world, whose process of natural production engages the lower part which, by this very unity of the soul, nevertheless refers to thought and reflection, so that Plotinian continuism makes it possible to integrate production—nature—with contemplation, which is no longer reduced to a pure theoretic activity that it would be possible to isolate. All that has just been explained can be understood in another way: it suffices to understand that *matter is not nature*, and that matter is not, *in itself*, *natural,* for matter is not, in itself, a process of production, but rather presents itself as a substrate destined to be informed by reasons. As a result, *the process of body formation is nothing other than the natural process itself,* and when a material body proves to be productive, it is insofar as it carries nature within it, and not insofar as it is materially constituted. Consequently, *by virtue of its naturalness, i.e. insofar as it is a moment in a process of production dependent on the vegetative part of the soul of the world,* the natural body can contemplate, production thus being part of contemplation. In short, such a statement presupposes that we do not see in bodies their *materiality*, but, on the contrary, their *naturalness* in the sense we have defined.

Behind the apparent complexity of what Plotinus describes, there is undoubtedly a kind of intuition of a quasi-obviousness: what he is trying to account for is quite simply the fact that *natural production does not take place blindly*. In other words, if nature presents itself to us in the form of a production process, then this process is ordered and rational: a blackbird, for example, produces a blackbird. This is why we need to think about the necessity of a *knowledge* of nature, of which the production process is only ever the expression. Something, to put it another way, *knows* what needs to be produced, and it becomes possible to go back from the product to the knowledge of the product, which is why it is no longer possible to exclude

production from contemplation: if I am indeed dealing with something determined among natural bodies, and if there is indeed a materialization of a Form via reasons, then it is because the *real as product expresses the structure of the real—reality—and, consequently, that the presence of this product is unintelligible outside of knowledge.* In short, what the real as product tells us is quite simply that *something knows what to produce.*

e) From bodies here to divine forms "over there

From the above, we understand that all Plotinian thought contains an effort to go from here below to "there", from the real to the structure of the real—reality—, from the world to the intelligible. Unlike the Stoics, who find everything they need to find here below and in matter, and who identify reality with reality without further ado, Plotinus remains faithful to Plato and seeks a non-material structuring of material bodies, a transcendent reality of reality. In many respects, what we have come to know as "nature" is one of the moments in this ascent *from the very fact that matter is not nature.* This makes it possible to understand the

Ennead V, 8, chapter 7 of which begins with the essential point that the being and determination of our world "comes from another[35]". This is an essential clarification, as it allows us to understand that, in Plotinus, a subtle dialectic is established between *ontological continuity and the maintenance of otherness*. In other words, *Plotinus is neither a monist nor a dualist, in the* sense that everything does not merge into a single nature—he is not a monist—although no unbridgeable break between two levels of being is established. The major difficulty of Plotinism is to identify this fragile ridge where it is established, which seeks to say that reality is not reality, that the very structure of things is not identified with them, while refusing to establish a gap between the things of the world and the reality of the world.

Turning towards "out there, towards that which is pure and everlasting, which is immortal and ever self-similar" evokes Plato, more precisely *Phaedo,*

---

35. Cf. in particular Plotinus, V, 8 [31], 7, 13-18, p. 100.

79 d. The soul, as a principle of movement, can drive motion towards the intelligible, and thus towards the eternal, towards that which escapes the corruption of time, towards that which is identical to itself and not corrupted by difference. This notion of "out there" [*ékei*], crucial for Plotinus, designates the totality of intelligible realities—immutable, universal and eternal realities—towards which the soul can therefore direct itself, and which rational thought makes it possible to conceive—not to possess. Plotinism is therefore an invitation to the soul to turn away from the body and turn towards itself, so that, probing its own origin, the soul rediscovers its intelligible provenance, which amounts to turning towards "over there". On this point, Plotinus is fully faithful to Plato who, in the *Phaedo*, had already described such a process, in which rational thought was the first stage in an ascent towards the intelligible.[36]

---

36. This state of the soul is what we call thought [phronesis]", in Plato, Phaedo, 79d, translation by Monique Dixsaut, Paris, GF, 1991. This state of the soul is what we call thought [*phronesis*]", *in* Plato, *Phœdon*, 79d, translation by Monique Dixsaut, Paris, GF, 1991, p. 242.

Chapter II:
The Intellect and Intelligibles.
Plotinian Ontology and Noetics

Although Forms, the intelligible and the Intellect were discussed at length in the previous chapter, their definition has not yet been precisely given. The time has come to understand what true being is, reality as such as a structuring of the real, i.e. the intelligible, but also to determine to what extent the world constitutes an otherness for the intelligible, even though Plotinus is not a true dualist.

To understand these elements, we need the concepts of reflection and image. Greek uses the term *eidolon*—literally "diminished form"—for reflection, and *eikon* for image. We know, moreover, that the world whose bodies are partitions always refers to more than itself, and that the soul of the world reflects the intelligible; as a result, the latter diffuses itself through reasons into matter, *naturally* producing bodies from the material substratum. A fundamental consequence of this is that, in Platonism and Neoplatonism, everything here below speaks to us of over there, everything here below evokes, in an admittedly imperfect, material and temporal form, the unchangeable, identity, provided we are not fooled by becoming, corruption and so on. There is certainly becoming and corruption, but they are not the last word in the world; such is the Plotinian teaching par excellence.

1) General Information on Intellect (*Noûs*)

At least since the pre-Socratics, Greek has had a fundamental term for Intellect, *noûs*. Diogenes Laërce (I, 35) tells us that Thales himself used it, while an analysis of the word reveals its kinship with thought, since *noûs* seems to be a contraction of *no-os*, *no* being the Greek root for everything related to thought. Hence *noésis*, *noéros* and *noêma*.

Plato makes the *noûs* the Intellect capable of grasping intelligibles, i.e. Forms. In other words, if we agree with Plato that Forms are the very structure of the real—reality—then the Intellect is that force of thought which alone is capable of knowing such a structure, which, in order to be precisely known, presupposes going beyond discursive thought, which remains trapped within a certain rational and linguistic development, and thus proves to be in part inadequate to truly grasp being itself. Nevertheless, through rational thought, the soul can help—as a springboard—to turn towards the intelligibles in order to know them, although the rational part of the soul is not, strictly speaking, the *noûs*.

Aristotle's revival of the Platonic scheme—decisive for Plotinus—is interesting. Indeed, it's a commonplace to recall the Stagirite's break with the Forms taken in their Platonic sense. While they were separate from sensible realities for the founder of the Academy, they structure material realities *from within* for Aristotle. This is also the case with the soul, which is the *eidos*—the form—of the living being, in the sense that it *gives* it *its shape*, i.e. structures it from within and organizes its materiality. Better still: for Aristotle, the thing is not the *eidos*, but the *eidos* makes the thing what it is; so a tree is a tree only by virtue of its *eidos*, by which it is a tree and not a tulip or a cow; the question then arises of what the soul can know of the tree: it can feel it, perceive it, form an image of it and know that image. But what is the basis of any image? On the visible appearance of the tree, which has this appearance (*morphè*) only by virtue of the *eidos*, an appearance that is nonetheless impure, since the *eidos* does not appear as such: it manifests itself only through the visible form (*morphè*) that it (the *eidos*) has organized.

The intellective soul must therefore go beyond the sensitive soul and think the *eidos* without the help of images, which presupposes that the eidos is the ideal correspondent of things. By the same token, the intellect would relate to these forms insofar as the latter are ideally accessible. But such an assertion raises an immense difficulty: is the *eidos* that organizes matter, and therefore transcends the soul, the same as that to which the intellective soul relates ideally? This raises the question: what is the intellect dealing with?

In Aristotle's fundamental treatise *On the Soul*, he adds that the Intellect "seems to be a different kind of soul, and it alone could be separated, like the eternal from the corruptible[37]. Let's understand this statement: it means that *the Intellect is not my intellect*, it is *the* Intellect, *the* noûs in general that my soul would reach when it becomes intellective. And Aristotle goes on to specify, again in *On the Soul*, that this intellective power is therefore fully itself only when it is separate, when it is not confused with the soul: "Only when it is separate is it precisely what it really is, and it alone is immortal and eternal[38]."

---

37. Aristotle, *On the Soul*, II, 2, 413b25, translation by Pierre Thillet, Paris, Gallimard, coll. Folio-essais, 2005, p. 108. Translation slightly modified.
38. *Ibid*, III, 5, 240a23, p. 167.

To be "immortal and eternal", intellective power must be devoid of matter, and must also always be in act, and therefore never in power. But under these conditions, what does the intellective soul think? It certainly thinks what is accessible to the Intellect, i.e. what we might call the intelligible. But what does Aristotle mean by the intelligible? As we've said, it's the forms, the *eidè*. How does the intellective soul relate to *eidè*? Aristotle uses a famous formula to answer this question: the soul is the locus of forms. And he adds: "It is not the whole soul that is this, but the intellective soul, and the forms there are not in entelechy, but in power[39]."

Here we see the real difference between Plato and Aristotle, which will play a role in Plotinus, namely that *the fundamental disagreement concerns the question of the soul*: for Plato, all living things need a soul to be in motion, including the *noûs* which, as a movement of intellection, requires animation, and therefore a soul. In other words, the divine in the Platonic sense does

---

39. *Ibid*, III, 4, 429a28, p. 164.

indeed have a soul. For Aristotle, on the other hand, God is pure Intellect "intelliging" itself—to which we'll return later—and thus excludes any form of soul, which always carries the threat of power. In short, for Plato, every intellect must be carried by a soul, for only the soul can *bring* a thought *to life*; consequently, divine *noûs* implies a divine *psuche*, and do Chapter II: the intellect and the intelligibles nc a living God. By contrast, the Aristotelian God has no soul, and his thought requires no psychological support, no *psyche*, since only the Intellect can be said to be immortal—i.e. divine. This is why we humans can only have forms in power, because we remain dependent on the movement of the intellective soul to relate to them, which, as a soul, maintains us in a certain power, a certain incompleteness, that distances us from the divine.

2) Plotinian Sense of *Intellect*

According to Porphyry's classification of the Enneads, what concerns the Intellect is grouped in the fifth Ennead. To fully understand what's at stake here, we need to bear in mind four crucial elements:

1 Plotinus is aware that the disagreement between Plato and Aristotle concerns the soul, and his entire analysis aims to find a median solution between his two principal masters.

2 Nevertheless, the central author for understanding Plotinus' defence of the very *nature of* the Intellect is Aristotle rather than Plato.

3 The foundation of the entire thesis is the *threefold identity of Intellect-Intelligibles (Forms)-being.* Being, Intellect and intelligibles, i.e. Forms, are the same thing. They are the same reality, i.e. the very structuring of reality by which the latter is what it is.

4 The Intellect, as identical with the intelligibles, with being, cannot be *my* intellect, it cannot be a personal intellect. If, then, being is the universal reality, and the Intellect is being, then the Intellect as universal intellect cannot be identified with the individual intellect, but must be open to universality, both as to subject and object: "[…] the Intellect is not the intellect of a single individual, but it is the intellect of all, and, being the intellect of all, it is

also the intellect comprehending all things[40]." This is reaffirmed in Treatise 49[41].

a) Aristotle's revival and its consequences

To understand Plotinus' position, we must first and foremost remember Aristotle's position. The soul has four faculties: vegetative (nutrition, production), sensitive (perception), appetitive (motor) and intellective. The human intellective soul is itself dual, and is distributed between a passive, or patient, intellect, called by Aristotle *noûs pathétikos*, and which, as its name indicates, receives forms from substances. In other words, to see the forms that structure the world, we need to receive them, we need a faculty of intellectual receptivity, and this intellectual receptivity is called the patient intellect. What's more, we need to understand what this means, namely that human intelligence is always waiting for its object, and can therefore only be exercised on the condition that it is exercised on an external reality: for a human being, "to

---

40. Plotinus, *Ennead* III, 8 [30], 8, 42-43, p. 43.
41. Cf. Plotinus, *Ennead* V, 3 [49], 3, 24-31, p. 327.

intellig" means to relate to an exteriority that makes a photographic impression on the patient intellect. The starting point of the human intellect is passive, and therefore imposes an exteriority, a dependence, but also a certain power. The human intellect is in power, since it does not always intellige; the sign of this is the fact that the human intellect requires a soul. In other words, the human intellect is a faculty of thought, a force that makes thought possible, but only makes it possible in power, as evidenced by the very fact that a soul is required to animate the movement of thought.

Once we have received the forms, we still need a kind of strength to extract them, to "abstract" them from the substance and contemplate them; we therefore need a second intellect, which Aristotle calls the "impassible intellect": its Greek name is interesting, as the privative "a" in *noûs apathès* indicates that it is named in *opposition to the first*, and that its first approach is a differential one. The impassive intellect is therefore first and foremost the intellect that differentiates itself from the patient intellect. In this respect, we must guard against the scholastic resemantization that has abundantly disseminated the notion of agent intellect, as if this qualification were present in Aristotle—which it clearly is not. We humans thus have two intellects, a passive one that receives forms, and an "impassive" one that exerts a force of abstraction from form and thus of *recognition of it.*

For reasons that would take too long to go into, but which have much to do with the absence of soul in the Aristotelian God—and, correlatively, his absence of life, despite the sometimes misleading translations— Aristotle is going to exclude all passivity from the latter, and therefore all patient intellect. In other words, as far as God is concerned, divine intelligence is pure, in act, and therefore complete, always conforming to what it has to be, and therefore always knowing, always *intelligible.* This means, first of all, that divine intelligence is always in the process of intelliging, and thus rules out the possibility of an intelligence which, at a given "moment", would not be intelliging. Intelligence and intellection as the act of intelliging are therefore

one and the same, since divine intelligence always intelliges. Furthermore, if divine intelligence always intellects, what does it intellect? What is the object of divine intellection? What is its *noeton*? Surely the Intellect as *noûs* can only deal with intelligibles; but are these *other* than the divine intellect? If so, then the divine Intellect would have to relate to something other than itself, and two things would have to be admitted: 1) The divine Intellect would have to be partly passive in order to receive the intelligibles it lacks; 2) If it lacks something, it would have to be in potency, for there would be an Intellect whose intellection would be incomplete, whose intellection could then not be in act.

By definition, this is impossible. So the divine Intellect is in act, it is always intellection, and what it intellects, the intelligibles, cannot *be* anything other than the Intellect itself. So Intellect (*noûs*) is identical to intellection (*noésis*), which is itself identical to the intelligible (*noéton*)[42]. To put it another way, it is only

---

42. We refer here to a canonical text by Aristotle: "Now Thought, that which is by itself, and sovereign Thought is that of the sovereign Good. Intelligence thinks itself by grasping the intelligible, for it

by contemplating forms—the intelligible—that God is himself, since contemplation of forms is intellection, which is itself Intellect. In God, then, *to intellig, is to be what he intelligentiates, and to be the very act of intellection.* To repeat with Aristotle, in *De l'âme,* "the subject who exercises intellection and the object of intellection are identical[43]."

Let's draw three conclusions:

1. Aristotle's God is not endowed with a personality or even an identity: he is not someone, but pure activity. He is the Intellect thinking always and eternally; the Intellect thinking the intelligibles, and the Intellect *being* the intelligibles, then the Intellect thinks itself, and divine beatitude can

---

becomes intelligible itself by coming into contact with its object and thinking it, so that there is identity between intelligence and the intelligible: the receptacle of the intelligible, i.e. of formal substance, is intelligence, and intelligence is in act when it is in possession of the intelligible. Hence actuality rather than power is the divine element that intelligence seems to contain, and the act of contemplation is perfect and sovereign beatitude", Aristotle, Metaphysics Δ, 1072b18-24, translation Tricot, Paris, Vrin, 1992, p. 681-682.

43. Aristotle, On the Soul, III, 4, 430a3-4, op. cit. p. 166.

be understood as intellectual self-contemplation. Better still: if the intelligibles are the forms that organize matter, and if the intelligibles are indistinguishable from God, then it's possible to say that the divine *noûs* is everywhere in the world, since the forms organize matter; if the forms are identical to the divine Intellect, then, mechanically, *finding the forms is tantamount to finding the divine noûs*, a consequence that Scholasticism eventually rendered invisible despite its obviousness with regard to Aristotelian conceptual logic.

2 Plotinus remains a Platonist, and so the Intellect that *is* the Forms is at the same time being, reality itself. For Plotinus, divine reality is both the Forms and the Intellect. So, to the Aristotelian equation, Plotinus adds divine being. And being, for a Platonist, is truth; it is what reality really is, and this is called truth, truth not being the adequation between a thought and the being that would be external to it, but truth is the being-thought identity that makes Plotinus take up the fundamental framework of Platonism for which it would make

no sense to distinguish reality from truth. Reality is the very truth of being. In more medieval terms, we could say that *being is essence*.

3   This equivalence is primarily polemical in scope: the medio-Platonists (Platonists of the first and second centuries AD) distinguished between Intellect and intelligibles. A philosopher like Alcinoos (circa 150), for example, considered intelligible ideas to be posterior to Intellect or, to put it more simply, that intelligible ideas were *produced* (and therefore different) by divine intellection. Against this medio-Platonic approach, Plotinus wishes to confer on intelligibles a kind of autonomous subsistence, as is forcefully indicated in Treatise 34.[44]

Nevertheless, such reasoning mechanically leads us to encounter a serious difficulty: the Forms are multiple, and the Intellect is one. How can we identify

---

44. "They [intelligible realities] do not exist because he who thinks, as soon as he thinks each of them, consequently gives them existence by this very thought. For it is not because one has thought what Justice can be that Justice exists; nor is it because one has thought what motion can be that motion exists", Plotinus, Ennead VI, 6 [34], 6, 7-10, p. 303-304.

a single element with multiple forms, when Intellect is presented as ontologically identical to the intelligible?

b) From content to identity

Most of the arguments that follow will have an Aristotelian resonance. To conceptualize the relationship between Intellect and the plurality of Forms, let's take a passage from Treatise 32:

"But if reflection is not introduced into him from outside, if he thinks something, it is by himself, and if he possesses something, it is by himself. And if he thinks by himself and from himself, he is himself what he thinks. For, if his reality and what he thinks were two distinct things, his reality would be, in itself unintelligible, and he would therefore once again be in power, not in act[45]."

The reasoning, inspired by Aristotle, is led by the absurd. Plotinus takes up the Aristotelian Intellect in act and not in power: as a result, the Intellect thinks what it has to think, and nothing intelligible remains

---

45. Plotinus, *Ennead* V, 9 [5], 5, 4-9, p. 203.

foreign to it. In other words, the Intellect in act thinks and knows all intelligible realities, i.e. everything that *is* in the Platonic sense of the term. But suppose now that these intelligible realities are other than the Intellect: this would imply that the Intellect, in thinking these realities, would not be thinking itself. It would therefore be in power with respect to itself, which is impossible for an Intellect in act. The Intellect therefore *contains* intelligible realities.

But why move from a relationship of *content to one of identity*? Why go from the idea that the Intellect *contains* the intelligibles to the idea that it *is* the intelligibles? And how can we understand the possibility of the multiple being identified with unity? Language is misleading here, because it invites us to represent the notion of content in a sensible way; and it's true that *in sensible realities, the container is not the content.* On the other hand, if we elevate ourselves to intelligible reasoning, and thus no longer reason from the point of view of what is felt, and *therefore partitioned*, but reason at the level of what is free of all sensible extent, then the situation is quite different. Imagine I take a hand and a glove: the glove contains the hand from the sensible point of view, and from this point of view the hand and the glove differ. In other words, they don't occupy the same place. If I now rise to the level of form, and ask myself why the glove can contain the hand, it seems to me that this is only possible because the glove and the hand have the same form, in both senses of the word "form". In other words, it is the identity of nature between the glove and the hand that makes possible their contact and, even more, their relationship of containment. The same applies to intelligible realities, which only have meaning as pure forms: the Intellect can only contain intelligibles if they have the same nature, if their nature is identical. Now, from the point of view of forms, having the same nature means being identical.

However, this reasoning does not remove all doubts: intelligible forms are indeed multiple, and they are all in the Intellect, but the Intellect is singular. So we have an Intellect that *is* reality, that is all things. To assert their identity is to assert the identity of oneness and multiplicity, which is particularly troubling. How can plurality be identical with oneness? There is a considerable difficulty here, which must be confronted as such. This difficulty is redoubled if we admit that this identity is perfect, for, in all rigor, if intelligible realities are the intellect, then *there are as many intelligible realities as there are intellects*, and the very notion of intellect must be open to multiplicity.

The key is to be found in Treatise 10, in particular chapter 4, which makes it possible to understand that the identity between being and *noûs* must be relativized, as Treatises 32 and 49 will later make clear. In a very subtle way, Plotinus introduces a dynamic relationship between Intellect and being that resolves all the difficulties and makes it possible to understand that, *while Intellect is identical in nature to the intelligibles—for the whole cannot differ from the parts— being and thought must nevertheless be maintained in their difference.* This is at the heart of chapter 4 of Treatise 10[46], which offers a remarkable text, very

---

46. Cf. Plotinus, *Ennead* V, 1 [10], 4, 21-39, p. 159-160.

Hegelian in essence, or very conducive to understanding what Hegel calls identity: if identity is a dynamic process, then it presupposes difference. Identity is affirmed by two *different* things. The affirmation of identity presupposes two different elements, which is perfectly understandable when I say "A=B". A and B are two different elements whose identity is affirmed. Hence, if I say that thought is identical to being, I must be able to think identity in difference, although I must at the same time think the process of identification, i.e. the movement by which two entities initially posited as distinct are identified. Consequently, as soon as I begin to think about intelligibles, I must have at my disposal a series of concepts without which they remain incomprehensible: difference, identity, movement. In short, what Plotinus understands is that *identification does not imply indistinction: thought and being can be distinguished even though they are identical.* In other words, the Intellect is divided into two branches: the very fact of thinking, the thinking subject, i.e. the intellection or intelliger, and what is thought, the object. To put it another way, the fundamental reality is the *noûs*;

but the *noûs*, as fundamental reality, is distributed into intellection and intelligible, *noésis* and *noéton* and, from this point of view, we can *distinguish* intellection from intelligible, the thinking subject from the thought object. To put it another way, fundamental reality is the *noesis* through which the coincidence of being and thought, which are nevertheless distinct, takes place.

c) Plotinus' legacy: Parmenides and Plato beyond Aristotle

In the very heart of the above, we hear the echo of Parmenides: taking up the famous paragraph 3 of Parmenides' *Poem*, which asserts that "the same is both thinking and being [*to gar auto noein estin te kai einai*][47]", Plotinus radicalizes his predecessor's statement. Whereas Parmenides asserted the non-separability of being and intellect, Plotinus goes infinitely further than non-separability, asserting the identity of being and intelliger, which belong to the same reality. But such a radicalization is only intelligible if we

___

47. Parmenides, *Poème*, § 3, edition by Jean Beaufret, Paris, PUF, coll. Épiméthée, 1955, p. 79.

distinguish Intellect from intellection or thought. The fundamental reality is the Intellect, the *noûs*. As such, it is unique, eternal and unchanging, and this unique reality will constitute what Plotinus calls a hypostasis. However, this hypostasis is distributed on the one hand according to thought, i.e. intellection, and on the other hand according to being, i.e. forms. Thus, to assert that being and thought—intellection—are identical is to assert that they have the same nature, the same essence, namely that of Intellect. "Intellect," writes Joachim Lacrosse, "is thus a single hypostasis, a single nature, but a single thing that immediately splits into being and intelliging [...][48]."

But Parmenides is not enough to account for what Plotinus is talking about; there are explicit references here to Platonic ontology, and thus to the *Sophist* as well as to *Parmenides*. In the *Sophist*, Plato already understands that the intelligible, though eternal, unchanging and removed from time, cannot be thought

---

48. Joachim Lacrosse, *op. cit.* p. 169.

in terms of identity alone. The most important genera [*génê*] [*mégista*]," writes Plato, "are certainly those we have just considered: being itself, rest and movement[49]. And the founder of the Academy immediately adds:

"Now, each of them is other than the other two, and even other than himself (…).

What have we just done, in turn, by saying "same" [*tauton*] and "other" [*hétéron*]? Are these two genres different from the other three, but still necessarily intertwined with them, and, therefore, our research had to focus on five and no longer on three, or are "same" and "other" just two names we unconsciously apply to the previous genres?[50]"

This is where the canonical texts on the fact that Platonism does not reduce the intelligible to identity are revealed, if only for a reason that has been studied at length, namely that the soul animates the intellect

---

49. Plato, *The Sophist*, 254d, translation by Nestor Cordero, Paris, GF, 1993, p. 171.
50. *Ibid*, 254d-e, p. 172.

and therefore movement is involved. On the other hand, in intelligibles, there can only be intelligibles; so if intelligibles have genus (*géné*), then genus are forms, are *eidè*. But, of course, not all *eidè* are genus. In any case, the *Sophist* lists five main genres: being, rest, movement, identity and difference. These genres are fundamental structures of being, are themselves undoubtedly forms—the debate on the subject far exceeds our purpose—and are intelligibles.

Plotinus takes up the five Platonic genres, and uses the following argument to demonstrate the necessity of these five genres: if there is a thinking subject, i.e. intellection, then there is movement; in this respect, Plotinus does not choose the Aristotelian option, since movement seems absolutely necessary to account for *all* intellection. On the other hand, the intelligible as an object of knowledge must be thought of as immobile, without which there would be no intelligible realities; it is therefore necessary to have "rest", without which there would only be becoming. On the other hand, the thinking subject that belongs to motion differs from the thinking object that belongs to rest; we therefore need "difference". But the *coincidence of being and thought* in terms of their nature presupposes "identity". Finally, the homogeneity of the intelligible world—that is, the *noûs* that knows itself in difference—presupposes the notion of "being", which completes the whole. We do indeed have an ontological unity of *noûs*, but this ontological unity does not exclude the plurality of kinds of being, and the *Sophist* provides Plotinus with the conceptual tools to think about this plurality.

Let's quickly conclude this second chapter. It's easy to understand that the Intellect, the *noûs*, may entail the coincidence of being and thinking, but it is not absolute identity, and therefore does not belong to the One, to put it in Plotinian terms. As a result, *to understand the* noûs *is to understand that it is not the supreme reality, since it contains traces of plurality and difference.* We must therefore go back to what Plotinus calls "the cause of thought" and the cause of being, namely the One.

Chapter III:
The Three Hypostases that Rank as Principles of Matter

If we look at the path we have travelled, we realize that a process of ascent is established from material bodies, which we have understood to be informed by reasons, which themselves are only thinkable in relation to the soul of the world that diffuses intelligibles in the form of reasons in matter, which presupposes going back to intelligibles, which leads to the discovery of the Intellect whose examination leads us to think the "cause", namely the One.

Such a journey is *ascensional* in nature, enabling the soul to leave the body and ascend to the cause of Intellect, i.e. to the One. For Plotinus, this ascent has a name: *epistrophè*, or "conversion", whereby the very fact of turning towards the One is tantamount to ascending towards the latter; thus, *conversion means gradually ascending towards the first principle of all things*, as described in chapter 4 of Treatise 32:

"It has been said that we must therefore go back to unity and true unity, which is not one as are other things which, while multiple, become one because they participate in the One—we must grasp what is not one by participation and what is no more one than multiple—and it has been said that the intelligible world and the Intellect are more one than the rest and that nothing is closer to the One itself, without yet being the One in all its purity. But what the pure, real and absolute One is, we long to contemplate now, if we can. Once we have reached this point, we must rush towards the One, and add nothing more to it[51].

---

51. Plotinus, *Ennead* V, 5 [32], 4, 1-9, p. 146.

1) From *Noûs* to *Hên*—and Back

The whole of Treatise 32, as well as a large part of Treatise 49, deals with the question: why is *noûs not* the supreme reality? This amounts to asking what is the relationship between being and the One. Here, we must start again from the question of *noûs* and understand exactly what its activity is, i.e. dig once more into the very meaning of the intellection of intelligibles. Let's not forget that, by its very nature, the Intellect is identical to intellection, which is itself identical to the intelligibles; therefore, *in knowing the intelligibles, the Intellect knows itself, knowledge of being being being knowledge of itself. But in order to know itself, the Intellect knows itself as noetic activity, as intellection. The Intellect thus relates to itself*—knows itself, since the only relation of which the *noûs* is capable is the noetic relation—*as intellection of intelligibles.* We thus have a perfectly coherent *three-term identity*, which reveals the crux of the problem: *to know is to split. To know implies a distinction between the knowing subject as intellection and the known object, in that all knowledge implies a distinction; hence, all knowledge is incompatible with a perfectly One reality, with the One. Herein lies the crux of the problem: the One inherently escapes all knowledge, for to know the One would be to make it an object of knowledge, and thus to introduce from the outset an object to be known and a knowing subject. The One is therefore, in principle, beyond all knowledge, all discourse, all noetics.*

But that's not enough; we need to go deeper into this point. What does the Intellect seek to know? Its very self. So, in a way, the very meaning of the *noûs'* approach is that of the One: to know Unity. But the very fact that this approach is noetic, and thus comes under the heading of knowledge which we have just shown to be structurally the bearer of scission, indicates a failure, and the proof of this failure is the introduction of difference and the kinds of being. In other words, the Intellect wants the One, but only falls back on itself, a failure that discovers being and the plurality of its kinds, but obscures the very thing towards which it turns, namely the One. The One is not noetically accessible, and nothing can be said about it.

Thus, as far as conversion is concerned, two essential things are now understood: the Intellect turns towards its higher principle, towards the One, because the Intellect knows that it comes from the One. But at the same time, it knows that it can say nothing about the One except that it is the supreme principle, and that the Intellect's self-knowledge is therefore a degraded image of the One, degraded because it is traversed by the difference and split between subject and object, between thinking and being. In short, the Intellect understands that it is not the supreme reality, and at the same time that the supreme reality does not belong to the Intellect.

But this perspective is solely that of conversion, i.e. of the ascent to the One. In Plotinism, however, there is a double movement that requires us to think in terms of procession (*proodos*), i.e. the diffusion of all things from the One. But this procession is mysterious from the outset, for while it seems understandable that the soul should seek to rediscover its origin through a series of conversions, the One as ultimate and perfect reality does not seem compatible with the production of multiplicity, from the Intellect to the profusion of matter. In this respect, the ultimate origin of all things is a real mystery.

We need to keep in mind something mentioned in the introduction, namely the concept of creation *ex nihilo*. In promoting this notion, certain Christians—not all, by any means!- did no more than provide an absurd solution to a problem that had been tormenting human intelligence for a very long time: how can there be multiple things when we admit that there is a single, perfect origin, i.e. one that is complete, lacking nothing and in particular not lacking in inconceivable otherness? Far from concepts involving creation—whether in Gnosticism or Christianity in general—Plotinus maintains a form of *continuity* between the One and that which immediately proceeds from it, namely the Intellect. The difficulty, then, lies in understanding why the One would emerge from itself or, more precisely, *diffuse itself in the form of the Intellect*, thus mechanically bringing about the scission inherent in any noetic act and losing itself in the multiplicity it has produced.

The only solution that can be adopted is that of a *superabundance of* the One, which, by a kind of surpassing of itself, would give itself *beyond itself by giving what it does not have*, requiring that there be precisely something *other* than the One. Thus, by superabundance, the One that does not have the Intellect would nevertheless produce the latter, thanks to which the One would give itself to itself in noetic form—we'll see at the end of the book that, from this angle, the One appears as Good. Added to this is the complex, almost cultural element that, for a Greek, a perfect reality cannot be sterile; in other words, *the perfection of a reality implies its productivity*. So, by the very fact that the One is supreme reality, it must produce something, but as a perfect unity, it can only produce in superabundance, the paradox being that, for the One, to produce is to lose oneself, for it is to lose fundamental unity and introduce duality.

Three crucial points of Plotinism are thus understood:

1 The very activity of the Intellect, namely intellection, is the search for unity: the Intellect wants to know itself, and this intellection indicates the principle from which the reality of the Intellect derives: therefore, if the Intellect seeks unity, it is because its principle is the One.

2 This search for unity fails because the Intellect knows itself only from the standpoint of plurality, i.e. from the standpoint of an intellection that relates to intelligibles, different elements that the Intellect grasps from the standpoint of identity and whose coincidence it ensures. As a result, the unity *known* by the *noûs* is not the One, and it immediately follows that *the One is beyond being and therefore beyond the knowable.* In this respect, it is not certain that Plotinus has a henology in the strict sense, since a henology would presuppose a discourse on the One or a science of the One; but this is impossible in principle, and therefore casts doubt on the presence of a henology; it would be more rigorous to speak of

a negative henology in the sense that nothing can be said of the One directly; we can only speak of the One through its production, namely the Intellect.

3 If the One can be neither knowable nor the object of discourse, this casts doubt on the fact that Plotinism is merely a philosophy; indeed, this crowning of Plotinian thought by a supreme reality that escapes all thought, even that of the divine Intellect, seems to play in favour of an unforeseen possibility, namely that Plotinism *is also* a mysticism that enables us to attain a *knowledge that would not be knowledge*[52] .

2) **Products of the One: From *Noûs* to Material Bodies**

Plotinus' ontology is *continuist*, revealing that everything, at different levels, proceeds at its own level from the original One. In other words, the One is the principle of all things, but this does not imply that all things have an identical relationship to the

---

52. Commentators such as Émile Bréhier have insisted at length on the mystical significance of Plotinism, notably in chapter 8 of *La philosophie de Plotin*. Cf. Émile Bréhier, *La philosophie de Plotin*, Paris, Vrin, 1990.

first principle. This notion of first principle implies an immediate understanding of what we call hypostases.

a) The notion of hypostasis

The term hypostasis appears in Plotinus' texts, but Porphyry, in his classification and titles, uses it differently from Plotinus. Hypostasis comes from the Greek *hupostasis*, literally meaning "that which stands beneath", whose strict Latin equivalent is "substance". The original Greek meaning of hypostasis is a medical one, designating a sediment in the urine or a blood deposit in the lungs. It's a very material meaning, not at all philosophical, and much more likely to refer to a self-sufficient deposit of matter. But this is hardly enough to understand its common usage. The term is found, for example, in Aristotle's classic meaning of "sediment, deposit". It has no philosophical meaning in Aristotle.

Plotinus, on the other hand, uses the word *hupostasis* one hundred and twenty times in twenty-eight treatises. If we unpack the term, *hup* refers to the idea of a support, a deposit or a bottom; then to the idea of sedimentation or concretion. This transformation implies the passage from a static to a dynamic stage. The term is also used to designate a deed of ownership to establish the authenticity of a possession, or even to designate the thing possessed itself as *actually* possessed. In the *Septuagint*, we find such uses. In the *Epistle to the Hebrews*, I, 3, we find the oldest philosophical use of the term, since the Son of God is called *charactere tos hupostaseos*. The term can also refer to firmness of character.

All in all, the notion of hypostasis conveys the idea of solidity, foundation, rootedness and *stability*. This is the sense in which Plotinus uses it, condensing in it both the firmness and the autonomous scope of a founding reality; in Plotinus, "hypostasis" basically means something like "existential foundation", and so to say of a reality that it has a hypostasis is to say that we are dealing with something really existing and consistent, in short with what the Latins would have called a *res.*

But the difficulty we are about to encounter lies in the fact that Porphyry will give the Treatises titles that will slightly inflect the question and reserve the term hypostasis for three levels of the One: the One itself, the *noûs* and the soul. Consequently, by reducing the extension of hypostasis to "ranks" of differentiated realities, Porphyry conferred on Plotinism a Trinitarian aspect that it did not necessarily have, or at least not to such an extent; the paradox is that the Trinitarian form will be part of what Christians will take up with the idea that the Triune God is distributed in three "persons" (Latin translation of the notion of hypostasis), namely the Father, the Son and the Holy Spirit.

Such a Trinitarian identification raises a number of difficulties, starting with that of the One: how can the One be a hypostasis when it is absolutely simple, beyond being and therefore impossible to say that it exists? Indeed, to ascribe an existential foundation to it constitutes a discourse on the One, and thus a *contradictio in terminis*. How can the One be *something*, some *res*, if it is absolutely simple? This is the problem of

Treatise 39, which, for the sake of consistency, refuses to ascribe any existence whatsoever to the One, since this would be to make the One fall back into being, and thus break the consistency of the discourse. In fact, this is precisely the problem of the *discourse* that can be held on the One: in all rigour, being beyond all noesis, all knowledge of the *noûs*, it can say nothing about it. However, given that we are dealing with a philosophy that discusses the nature of things, it is all *the* more appropriate to talk about it, since if the One did not exist in any way, we could not make it a supreme principle; it must therefore exist, but not in the sense understood by the Intellect, not in the sense of being[53]. There is thus what Plotinus calls a "kind of existence" (cf. Treatise 39, 7, 47), *he hoion hupostasis autoû*, i.e. something in him that makes him be, but not in the sense of being as known to the Intellect. In many respects, then, it is a mistake to say of the One that it *is*, but it is an *absurdity* to deny it any form of existence.

---

53. Jean-François Pradeau rightly says that if you can't talk *about* the One, you can talk *about* the One.

Absurdity, we write, in that the ground on which the necessity of the One is felt—at least from a philosophical point of view—is a purely *logical* one. Indeed, the One is indeed the first hypostasisbut it is so in a sense that we cannot grasp, although we can grasp the *necessity that there be a first hypostasis articulated around the supreme unity*[54]. The necessity of affirming the One thus does not imply knowledge of the latter, but avoids the ruinous self-validation of the Intellect by itself. Moreover, the One obeys a kind of causal process: a cause must make it "be"; but this cause can only be itself, without which it would not be the One; consequently, the One is in a way *causa sui*.[55, 56]

---

54. Cf. in particular Plotinus, Ennead V, 4 [7], 1, passim.
55. On the importance and scope of this notion, cf. Jean-Marc Narbonne, "Plotinus, Descartes et la notion de *causa sui*", *Archives de Philosophie*, vol. 56, no 2, 1993, pp. 177-195; Thierry Gontier, *Descartes et la causa sui. Autoproduction divine, autoproduction humaine*, Paris, Vrin, 2005 and Thibaut Gress, *Descartes et la précarité du monde. Essai sur les ontologies cartésiennes*, Paris, CNRS Éditions, 2012.
56. Jean-François Pradeau sums up the two theoretical gains of the One, despite the difficulties it raises: "It also means that being and knowledge are ontologically founded, so that they are no

The Intellect is the second hypostasis; the *noûs* is therefore the second reality, a reality whose activity consists in knowing, and whose object *is* the intelligibles. Finally, there is a third reality, which is not the Intellect, but the soul, whose principle is nevertheless the Intellect, since the principle is the origin. The Intellect thus appears as the pivot of the hypostases, for it is both the product of the One and the producer of the soul.

b) From the soul as hypostasis to the plurality of souls

The soul is the third hypostasis, the third level of stable reality, the third level of solidity. This raises the question of the plurality of souls, or more precisely, the plurality of the *meaning of* the soul. The soul we're going to talk about first is the soul as hypostasis, as

---

longer in a situation of self-confirmation, as is the case in a theory of knowledge that expects the intellect to confirm the existence or truth of what is, nor in the situation where one would escape the other, as is the case in a theory of knowledge that would assert that the intellect may not grasp being", Jean-François Pradeau, *Plotinus, op. cit,* p. 124.

fundamental reality, as the product of Intellect, and this soul is necessarily unique as an existential level.

Treatise 27, fundamental to understanding Plotinus' thinking on psychology, is unequivocal: there is the soul as hypostasis, and there are other souls, whether world souls or individual souls, which is to say that *the soul as hypostasis is not the world soul*. For," writes Plotinus, "it is because all souls come from the same Soul, from which the soul of the world also comes, that there is sympathy between them. Yes, it has been well explained that there is both a single soul and several souls[57]."

In fact, Plotinus explained that the soul as hypostasis cannot be the soul *of something*; in other words, the soul as hypostasis has no complement, because it is a hypostasis, a substance, and in this case cannot become the attribute of something else. Indeed, it would be contradictory to have a substance that supports itself and at the same time be the support of *something else*. This is

---

57. Plotinus, IV, 3 [27], 8, 3-4, p. 74.

the argument of chapter 2, in which Plotinus explains that individual souls and the soul of the world belong to the same species, namely the soul as hypostasis, for "the soul in its totality is not the soul of something, since it is of course a substance, admitting that there is a soul which is in no way the soul of anything, and souls, all of which are the souls of something, and which become so at a given moment by accident[58]." Here Plotinus returns to the Aristotelian argument in the *Categories* that a substance cannot be predicated of something else, on pain of no longer being a substance; something is a substance, but a substance is not the substance of something, without which the substance would become an accident and no longer be a substance.

We thus have a kind of fundamental existential level that is the soul as hypostasis, as substance, which is in short a "universal" soul, while all other souls, including the soul of the world, are "parts" of it, provided of course that we guard against the material vision of parts which are not, in this case, a sharing. In short,

---

58. *Ibid*, 2, 5-11, p. 63.

this is tantamount to asserting that all souls belong to a soul of the same kind.

As a result, the regime of souls in relation to the soul as hypostasis is reminiscent of the regime inherent in the Intellect and the relation of intelligibles to it. Remember that the Intellect as a fundamental reality was distributed into intellection and intelligibles, into thinking and being; the same applies to the soul as hypostasis, which is distributed into world soul and individual souls, as Plotinus summarizes at the end of chapter 5 of Treatise 27:

"So here's the summary of the thesis. Souls arise from a single Soul, and these souls arising from a single Soul are many in the same way as the Intellect. It is in the same way that they are partly divided and partly not. And the Soul that remains there is the single reason of the Intellect, and it is from this Soul that the particular and immaterial reasons are derived, just as is the case there[59]."

---

59. *Ibid*, 5, 15-18, p. 70.

Since we've understood that Plotinus spoke sometimes of the soul as hypostasis, sometimes of souls, we must now insert this distinction into the questions of conversion and procession; strictly speaking, the general movement of the soul concerns that of the soul as hypostasis; it is this that we must in fact think of according to two movements, on the one hand according to the movement of conversion—*epistrophè*—and, on the other, according to the movement of procession. Moreover, like the Intellect, and as a perfect reality, the soul must be both the product of the Intellect and the *producer of* something. But what does it produce, since according to Porphyry's classification there are only three hypostases, and therefore no hypostasis after the soul?

Before answering, let us understand that the division we made between the world soul and individual souls is only intelligible to the extent of the soul as hypostasis. Moreover, the soul as hypostasis seems to contain the very reason of the Intellect; but it cannot contain the reason of all individuality; as a result, we are brought back to the duality of the *Logoi* we spoke of in the first chapter: there are the "pure" reasons, i.e. exclusively inherent in the Forms, and there are the individuating reasons that will require the intervention of the particular souls that will be their vehicles. Finally, let's also remember that the soul in the Plotinian sense possesses several faculties or levels: vegetative, sensory, appetitive and rational. All these "parts" are linked, and it is this very link that makes it possible for the soul as hypostasis to ascend from the bottom to the top and find the Intellect as principle; nevertheless, it seems that this tripartition of the soul is found in all souls of the same species; in other words, the soul as hypostasis is like the *boss of souls*, so that the psychological structure is given by the hypostasis while being found in every soul, be it the world soul or individual souls. Hence, the relationship of the soul to the Intellect is the same as that of souls to the intellects "because they are the 'reasons' of these intellects and are more deployed than the latter are [...][60]."

---

60. *Ibid*, 5, 9-10, p. 70.

c) Conversion and procession: the double movement of the soul

The aim of the present development is first and foremost to identify the function of the upper part of the soul, i.e. its rational part; we have already indicated that *logos* presupposes content, and the very development of content makes discursive thought possible. This is fundamentally the exercise of the upper part of the soul. In so doing, the soul seeks to think intelligibles, forms, but cannot grasp them intuitively; it is therefore always separated from intelligibles by discursion, by *dianoia*, by *logos*, which means that rational content is both what leads to intelligibles and at the same time what separates it from them. Analogously, this is understood in terms of the path and the arrival; it is impossible to reach a certain point without taking a certain path, but the very fact that there is a need to travel the path signals how far we are from the point of arrival. In this respect, the soul's conversion to the Intellect enables it to turn towards the latter, which reveals itself to be its principle; but if the soul recognizes its principle, it does not, for all that, access the intelligibles in the same way as the Intellect: it only accesses them by discursive means, and thus keeps itself at a distance from them—the distance of reasoning.

The soul is thus described as "an image of the Intellect[61]": the *psyche* is *eikôn* of the *noûs*, which is to say that it *is* the Intellect while not being it. How can we resolve this paradox? For Plotinus, all that is perfect must be productive, since perfection cannot be deprived of generation. The Intellect must therefore, by virtue of its very perfection, generate something, but this something has a hybrid status: as the product *of the Intellect*, it is an indeterminate, unlimited, perfect reality that extends the nature of the Intellect. But *as a product*, it is an inferior reality, an *image* (*eikôn*) determined and limited by its principle: "because it is an image of him, it is inferior to him, and for the same reason it is unlimited, even if it is limited by what he has engendered and is as it were conformed by him."[62]

---

61. Plotinus, *Ennead* V, 1 [10], 3, 7, p. 157.
62. *Ibid*, 7, 40-42, p. 165.

This accounts for the soul's conversion to Intellect; but the soul, as the image of Intellect, therefore possesses remnants of perfection; and as such it cannot be sterile and must produce. The question is: what does the soul produce, even though, according to Porphyry's classification, no hypostasis, and therefore no stable existential level, can proceed from the soul? We know part of the answer: the soul, as the soul of the world, is at the origin of Nature, it is *natura naturans*. But nature is not exactly the same thing as matter, since nature is a dynamic process by which reasons inform matter, a process that presupposes the presence of matter that is, as it were, always already there; but in Plotinian logic, everything has to be produced, so we have to ask where matter comes from. And here we discover the soul's second productive activity, namely the production of matter.

We need to understand both the context and the inner motives of this reasoning. The context is that of the defenders of Gnosticism who, judging matter to be evil, assert that it can only have been produced by an

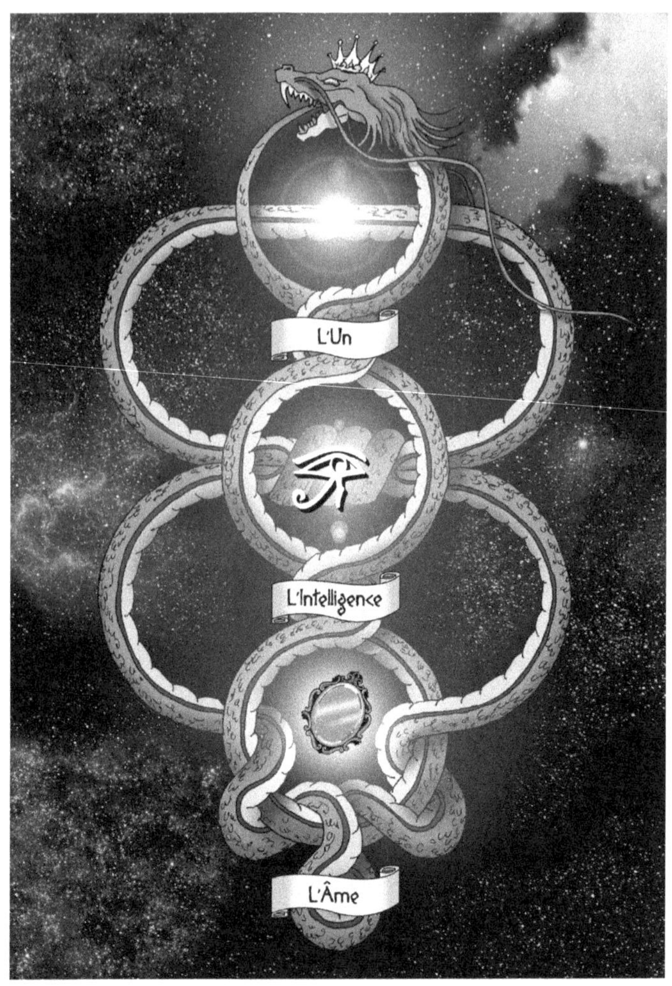

L'Un
L'Intelligence
L'Âme

evil principle that, depending on the author, will be called an "evil demiurge", a "wicked god", or even Yahweh in the Marcionite approach, for whom Yahweh as creator God is an evil God counterbalanced by the God of love of the New Testament texts. Whichever version of Gnosticism we choose, we're dealing with a dualism opposing the principle from which *noûs* comes, to the one from which matter proceeds, a dualism that creates a kind of irreducible split at the very heart of being, since it introduces *two Intellects*, thus splitting the second hypostasis[63]. This is exactly what Plotinus intends to refute, for by virtue of his continuism, he can only oppose all forms of dualism head-on, in order to make the continuity established from the One to matter conceivable. The aim of Treatise 33, which is directed against the Gnostics, is to reject Gnosticism on fundamental grounds, which presupposes the rejection of

---

63. Cf. *Ennead* II, 9 [33], 2, 1-4: "Therefore, among the principles of there, we must not add other realities, nor make superfluous distinctions that these realities do not admit. On the contrary, we must posit one and the same Intellect, which remains identical to itself, which does not incline in any direction and which imitates its father as far as it is possible for it to do so."

any form of condemnation of the world by virtue of the very continuity of the procession that forbids the material world to be seen as an evil element:

"Nor should we concede that our world has a bad origin on the pretext that there are many painful things in it. For this is the judgment of people who make too much of the world, insofar as they judge our world to be identical with the intelligible world, whereas it is the image of it[64]."

Playing on the terrain of Gnosticism, Plotinus turns them on their head in that he sees in their reflection a form of intellectual alienation from the world which, instead of teaching them to see what the world is the reflection or image of, imprisons them in it by virtue of the belief that the world would be the intelligible itself or, to put it another way, the real would be reality. However, in the very logic of Plotinian procession, the Intellect produces the soul, which in turn produces

---

64. Plotinus, *Ennead* II, 9 [33], 4, 22-26, p. 207.

matter, so that the material world is a transitive image—through the transitivity of the soul—of the Intellect. And Plotinus adds: "What other image could there be of the intelligible that is more beautiful?[65]"

That said, the fact that matter or the material world is not to be condemned does not explain why it proceeds from the soul, or why the latter necessarily produces something beyond itself. To account for this procession, we need to go to the very heart of the notion of production or generation as elaborated by Plotinus, who uses the crucial term *tolma*, which in Greek means "audacity" or "boldness", to think of the split implicit in any generation between producer and product, between progenitor and generated. In the case of the soul as hypostasis, this boldness consists in wanting to conquer its autonomy, its independence from the principle, in such a way that it turns the movement of which it is the principle into a lever to free itself from its own origin—hence from the Intellect.

---

65. *Ibid*, 4, 26-27, p. 207.

A complex pattern emerges here, in which the soul's process clearly proceeds from its will: it does *not suffer from outside* the situation that is now its own. Proceeding from the intelligible, which is divine, it is itself divine in nature, at least in part, and cannot therefore be deprived of will, i.e. of the necessity that impels it to be itself: "since it is the god of last rank, it is by a free inclination, and to exercise its power and put in order what comes after it that it comes here[66]."

The soul's animation of matter is not, therefore, to be seen as an unjust and suffered decline: it is the product of a *will on* the part of the soul, which is thus led to become autonomous and, in so doing, to upset the ontological order by splitting the principle—intelligible realities—from what it has generated—the soul. This is an *ethical* problem, in the sense that this process involves ambiguous *voluntary behavior*: strictly speaking, *this will is not a choice*, but an *unconstrained movement*. In other words, the soul does not undergo

---

66. Plotinus, *Ennead* IV, 8 [6], 5, 26-27, p. 248.

this descent, but neither does it choose it. The break and split are therefore voluntary only in a very limited sense, that of an ontological necessity that does not, however, constrain the movement from the outside. Here, we need to clarify the meaning and, as we said in the introduction, recall the obvious fact that the Greeks were not prisoners of the individualist paradigm, which enabled them to understand that a free will is not a matter of individual choice, but rather of conformity to the very nature of a reality. To put it very clearly, the soul's voluntary emancipation from the intellect proceeds from its will without being a choice[67] "since the voluntary is precisely included in the necessity[68]". This is easy to understand, as long as we bear in mind that, for Plotinus, necessity refers to the very nature of things: *that which follows from the nature of an entity is necessary.* As for the will, it is not a faculty, but *that which is not constrained by an external element*; under

---

67. On this delicate question, cf. Denis O'Brien, "Le volontaire et la nécessité: réflexions sur la descente de l'âme dans la philosophie de Plotin", *Revue philosophique de la France et de l'Étranger* 167.4 (1977), pp. 401-422.
68. Plotinus, Ennead IV, 8 [6], 5, 2-3, p. 247.

these conditions, what is voluntary is that which is carried out in accordance with the nature of a thing; and to be carried out in accordance with the nature of a thing is a necessary realization, so the voluntary is included in necessity. Therefore, *to say that the soul voluntarily frees itself from the Intellect is to say that it belongs to the very nature of the soul to autonomize itself as a hypostasis—as an autonomous existential foundation—and to produce a material world that it organizes.* By becoming autonomous, the soul acts in accordance with its nature, and is therefore not subject to any external constraint, and therefore acts according to a will that is free because it is not constrained, although it is required by its own nature. In short, and to put it with Plotinus, "it is necessary by virtue of an eternal law of nature that it undergoes and produces these inferior realities [...][69]."

But this is not enough, for if we understand the need for the soul to free itself from the Intellect, we still need

---

69. *Ibid*, 5, 11-12, p. 247.

to determine the reason why this emancipation takes the form of the production of matter. Admittedly, its link with perfection helps to answer this question, in that it reminds us that every perfect entity must be productive; but this is not enough to account for the entire problem. Let's reason by absurdity and ask ourselves what the absence of matter would mean for the soul, which is tantamount to asking what meaning there would be in a world whose existence is only intelligible. First of all, this would mean that the soul would be indistinguishable from the Intellect, that it would lose its own reality since, like the Intellect, it would contemplate the intelligible; yet, in Plotinus' processual scheme, the soul's existence as an autonomous reality is necessary, and therefore voluntary. Once autonomized, the soul needs to exercise its perfection, but it cannot exercise it on intelligible realities: it must therefore *necessarily* give itself a non-intelligible substratum on which it can exercise its own intelligible activity, the image of which it retains by virtue of its origin. In other words, matter is what the soul gives itself to objectify its own power. In short, *without matter, the soul's own power could not be* actualized:

"The soul itself would have been unaware of the things it possesses, since they would not even have come out to manifest themselves. For the act reveals everywhere the power which without it would remain totally hidden, as inapparent, and non-existent since it would never have any real existence[70]."

d) Plotinian paradoxes

This first approach has enabled us to determine the *nature of* the soul: originating from intelligible realities, it retains their nature. Strictly speaking, then, *the soul is an intelligible reality*, and as such, it is endowed with a will that is not synonymous with choice, but rather the sign of an internal necessity, namely to conform to its own nature, which leads it to free itself from its own origin. The paradox is that the exercise of will, which leads it to be as close as possible to its nature, distances it from its nature; its audacity (*tolma*) distances it from its own nature, splits it from itself and opens it up to otherness, i.e. opens it up to that which is

---

70. *Ibid*, 5, 32-36, p. 248.

not intelligible, thus linking it to material and sensible realities. Consequently, the soul is that divine reality which has *lost its unity*: *its dilection no longer coincides with its origin*, even though only its origin accounts for this discrepancy, so that what it is directed towards does not correspond with its nature. A fragmented reality, it is split between its upper part, which reminds it of its origin, and its lower, audacious part, which alienates it from the material realities it has produced. And the more daring it is in its desire to free itself, which *is the very heart of its nature as a hypostasis inherited from the Intellect*, the more it descends into matter "through its desire for what is inferior[71]".

But, as Plotinus sees everything as continuist, this openness to otherness, inscribed in the very audacity of the soul, is partly filled by the *Logoi*, since matter is immediately informed by the rational expression of intelligibles, of Forms. As a result, a double paradox emerges in the soul's relationship with matter: on the

---

71. Plotinus, *Ennead* V, 2 [11], 1, 27, p. 218.

one hand, it is because the soul is divine in nature and related to the Intellect that it can distance itself from it, since it possesses, by virtue of its divine and hypostatic nature, an audacious will that leads it to seek its autonomy, so that the production of matter is the paradoxical expression of the soul's divine nature ; on the other hand—and this is the second paradox—the matter produced by the soul, which seems to express a lively otherness towards the divine, is at the same time destined to receive the intelligible via reasons, via seeds, so that the soul fills the gap it has opened, thus ensuring the continuity of things, and diffusing into formless matter the form enabling it to become a body.

In this way, we understand that matter is not, in itself, anything determinate; it is never anything but privation—*steresis*—and can never have a precise content. It is never more than the receptacle of reasons expressing intelligibles, which amounts to saying that *matter has two definitions*: it is first substratum, then privation; substratum because it is destined to receive reasons in order to form bodies, but privation because,

in itself, it is nothing determined, it is not a fundamental reality, it is not a hypostasis[72].

The soul produces matter for two reasons: firstly, because it must necessarily exert its power on something that is not intelligible, matter being that chaotic substratum totally devoid of intelligibility; and secondly, because it must know its own thought, which is to say that by organizing matter intelligibly via reasons, it mediately knows what it possesses. Two elements are therefore distinguished: *matter*, the raw element, the substrate produced by the soul, and *bodies*, the organized products of matter by the soul and in this respect intelligible. Being organized, the body—and not matter—is the immediate, objectified manifestation of the soul, which is intelligible by nature. Bodies are therefore a transitive pathway to intelligible realities, and the world—not as a material entity, but as an organized corporeal entity—is a means for the soul to rediscover its intelligible origin, even though the Intellect does not know bodies.

---

72. Cf. Plotinus, *Ennead* II, 4 [12], 14, *passim*.

Chapter IV:
Plotinian Living and Feeling

To understand Plotinism, as Plotinus invites us to do, is first of all to assimilate the meaning of a certain number of concepts that need to be defined; but nothing would be more abstract than to leave it at that, and not to give a sense of what it's all about in an empirical life, as this would be to produce an exposition condemned to remain external to the subject who discovers it. In this final chapter, then, our ambition is not to develop new concepts, but rather to address the existential and empirical aspect of Plotinism in the way of life it implies. In this respect, we would almost go so far as to say that, like many ancient and even modern philosophies, Plotinus' thought is *felt* before it is understood; it is *experienced* before it is theorized, even though, since this way of feeling has been lost, it has become necessary to begin with a theoretical approach. But we must not forget that the practical dimension of Plotinus' philosophy was placed first by Porphyry—such is the purpose of the first Ennead—and that this seems to indicate the very evidence of its content, progressively justified and fortified by an ontology and a noetics. We, on the other hand, are condemned to follow the opposite path, otherwise Plotinian ethics and its related way of feeling the world would seem particularly gratuitous.

1) From Evil to Bad, or from Matter to a Look at Matter

Plotinus' condemnation of Gnosticism, and hence his profound refusal to burden matter with an intrinsic negativity, must always be borne in mind. Plotinus is not dismayed by the presence of matter, and even makes it a product of the soul, into which the reasons for the formation of bodies can be poured. As a result, the body is not condemned either, since it is the very objectification of reasons as developed or explicit images of the Forms[73].

Nothing could be further from the truth than to make Plotinus' version of Neoplatonism a rejection of bodies and matter, or a one-sided condemnation of the world and all that it implies. However, as Plotinus is a thinker of subtlety, it is important to understand that, while matter and bodies are not inherently evil—without which Plotinus would fall back into Gnosticism—they must, on the other hand, be viewed in a way that does *not reduce them to what they appear to be*. In other words, *matter and bodies* change their meaning according to how we look at them, and if we only see matter as matter, or bodies as bodies made up of matter, then they become traps, alienating the soul from its own product. If, on the other hand, matter and material bodies appear to the eye as an *opportunity* to probe their origin and

---

73. Jean Derrida thus dates the emergence of a genuine reflection on the body, caught up in a back-and-forth with the soul, to Neoplatonism. Cf. Jean Derrida, *La naissance du corps (Plotinus, Protius, Damascius)*, Paris, Galilée, 2010.

principle, then they can serve the soul as a means of ascending towards fundamental reality.

Here we return to the importance of reflection and model, which ultimately constitutes the description of a certain *gaze* by which everything, especially the body, is to be viewed as the image or copy of a higher model, and not as a self-sufficient, exclusively material individuality. The general principle is set out on several occasions, most notably in Treatise 31, in an interpretation of the Demiurge's production of the world in Plato's *Timaeus*: "he [Plato] wished to show how pleasing the beauty of the model is. Whenever we admire a thing made after another, the admiration is in fact for the thing after which the first was produced[74]."

In conceptual terms, this gaze, which invites us to see in everything more than itself, or more precisely, its origin, is called *conversion*. In this respect, the conversion of the soul concretely designates a way for

---

74. *Ennead* V, 8 [31], 8, 9 13, p. 102-103.

the latter to look at the world, to find itself in it, and thus to turn towards itself, and to go back to the very reality of reality, to the intelligibles, to the Intellect and to the One through mystical union. Treatises," writes Pierre Hadot, "are spiritual exercises in which the soul sculpts itself, i.e. purifies, simplifies and rises to the plane of pure thought, before transcending itself in ecstasy[75]."

On the other hand, what can be called vice can only be attributed to the weakness of the soul, incapable of conversion and indulging in the dispersion of the world, seeing in it nothing more than a multitude of self-sufficient and desirable *realities*; However, to adopt such a view is to fall into a certain oblivion or occultation, namely the oblivion of the very *origin* of material bodies, and therefore the oblivion of the chain of being which, distributing itself in the soul and then in matter, spreads a certain continuity at the very heart of otherness. In this respect, to allow oneself to be

---

75. Pierre Hadot, *Plotinus or the Simplicity of Looking*, Paris, Gallimard, coll. Folio-essais, 1997, p. 21.

seduced by the world is to forget that the latter is an *otherness* relative to being, and thus to forget that the world only makes sense relationally, to the benefit of a kind of reification of the latter. Plotinus repeatedly insists that, while evil is indeed non-being, it is not evil in the sense of nothingness, but in the logical sense of negation, i.e. in the sense that non-being is *not* being:

"Non-being is not, however, total non-being, but only that which is something other than being. [...]. This non-being is the totality of the sensible, as well as all the affections related to it [...][76]."

Non-being is therefore not nothingness, and negation is not contrariety, but otherness in relation to reality. However, non-being—and therefore evil—is not evil in itself, otherwise it would be tantamount to condemning all matter and all bodies on principle, something that Plotinian ontology as a whole forbids; the difficulty is then considerable, as it consists in elucidating the

---

76. Plotinus, *Ennead* I, 8 [51], 3, 6-10, p. 41.

possibility that evil as non-being is nevertheless not absolutely evil; In other words, matter is evil in the sense of non-being, i.e. matter is indeed the deprivation of being and thus of the Good—the Good being understood here in the sense of the absolutely desirable—but, in the absolute, it is not evil in that it is not to be condemned on principle. To put it another way, if matter is evil, this is not enough to condemn it, for it only becomes truly evil through a gaze: *the gaze on matter, and thus on evil as non-being, is the very locus of the ethical problem, in that the vicious gaze is the one that forgets the fact that matter is non-being.* In other words, vice is never more than the transformation of non-being into being by the gaze, and is therefore never more than the absolutization of a relative element, an occultation that occurs when the rational part of the soul finds itself so confused and seduced by matter as such that "it finds itself prevented from *seeing* because it is affected [...][77]." In short, Plotinus is trying to say that, without matter, the very notion of evil would be

---

77. *Ibid*, 4, 18, p. 44. Emphasis added.

meaningless in that matter *is* evil, even though the *evil of evil only emerges through a gaze that sees in matter only matter*—instead of seeing in it non-being and thus the other of being.

Finally, the reason why the soul's gaze becomes vicious is explained by the latter's weakness ceasing to fight against what is lowest in it; affections and sensations overwhelm it, and it no longer produces the effort to distinguish itself from them through rational exercise: "in reality, we perform bad deeds because we give in to the worst parts, just as in matters of sensation, common sense can perceive something false before reason has conducted its examination [...][78]." Matter is thus evil as non-being, as deprivation of being and therefore of Good, but action becomes ethically evil only when the soul looks at this same matter and obscures its origin; such obscuring or forgetting can be explained by a certain weakness of the soul which, renouncing its higher part, renouncing reasoning, allows itself to be

---

78. *Ennead* I, 1 [53], 9, 10 11, p. 195.

submerged by its vegetative and sensitive part, which submerges the exercise of reason.

This is where the difference between evil and acting badly comes into play, for acting badly means first and foremost a weakness of the soul in relation to matter, and thus an absence of virtue conceived as strength. The gods, on the other hand, have a virtuous, i.e. strong, soul, which protects them against any weakness with regard to the material composition of their bodies, and Plotinus can easily conclude in these terms:

"Although matter is present in the sensible gods, there is no evil in them: there is not in them that vice which we find in men [...][79]."

Finally, let's note that the Intellect is never concerned by vice, and is strictly "infallible[80]".

---

79. Plotinus, *Ennead* I, 8 [51], 5, 30-32, p. 46.
80. Plotinus, *Ennead* I, 1 [53], 9, 13, p. 195. For more on this subject, see Jean Trouillard, "L'impeccabilité de l'esprit selon Plotin", in *Revue de l'histoire des religions*, vol. 143, no. 1, 1953, pp. 19-29.

2) Subjectivity and Ipsity

The preceding paragraph invites us to think about *who* exactly is in a position to adopt a certain view of the world, and thus either fall into vice, or convert and ascend via rational thought to reality. In short, it's a question of identifying both the subject of conversion and its *identity*. These two questions are those of subjectivity, on the one hand, and ipsity, on the other. As far as subjectivity is concerned, it would be tempting to say that the soul is the very principle of the subject, that the individual soul *is* subjectivity, and is therefore the subject of rational thought as much as of the affections. Strictly speaking, it is indeed the soul that thinks, that animates thought, but that also supports affections and sensations.

The fact that it is the soul that thinks also raises a serious difficulty, since the higher part of the soul is certainly rational, but is therefore confined to a discursive or *developed* approach to the intelligibles; In other words, *the rational soul relates to intelligibles only under the aspect of* logos, develops a discourse about them, but in the strict sense *this discourse is not perfectly in line with what it is the discourse of*; the discursion of the rational soul presents in the very deployment of language a reality which, as such, is not extended and therefore not developed. In short, *ordinary language is unable to express being*, and if the rational part of the soul leads us to it, it fails to *express it*, because being cannot be expressed. It's worth noting here what we've mentioned at length in previous chapters, namely the fact that all *dianoia*, all discursive knowledge that calls upon the *logos*, institutes a *gap* with the object thought about and cannot be the last word of thought; consequently, *the knowledge that the Intellect can have of itself as intellection of the intelligibles is intuitive, direct, immediate*, whereas the rational thought of the soul introduces, between itself and the intelligibles, the *logos* itself as rational discourse. To put it another way, as long as the soul reasons, it cannot intuit the intelligibles, which are only fully given to the Intellect in a self-intuition; consequently, the only way for the soul to have an authentic *noesis* of the intelligibles is to unite with the Intellect in order to know being *from within and without distance,* which implies that the soul's union with its principle—the Intellect—is already a certain form of spiritual union.

The problem, then, is to determine whether personal identity is diluted in such a union, which presupposes resolving the soul's relationship to ipsity. This is an extremely complicated question, which can only be touched upon and pointed out. Ipsity, which refers to personal identity, raises the classic question of individuation, i.e. why there are individualities, each distinct from the others. Plotinus poses the question on several occasions, notably in the decisive Treatise 27, and asks himself in these terms:

"But how will there still be a soul that is yours, a soul that is this individual's, and a soul that is another[81]?"

It's a daunting question, and its very formulation reveals all its pitfalls: the soul is not exactly

---

81. *Ennead* IV, 3 [27], 5, 1 2, p. 69.

individuality. The individual as the result of individuation—so this tree, that man, this planet, etc.—engages the reason for individuation and raises many problems. Firstly, as a fundamental reality, as a hypostasis, there is only one soul, and it's hard to understand how individuation can take place from a single soul. What's more, since Plotinus' entire effort consists in going back to the intelligible, after having shown that matter is a kind of indeterminate product, an otherness of being that is itself deprived of Forms even though it is informed by reasons, it follows that it is impossible to make matter the principle of individuation. In other words, neither the soul, which as a fundamental reality is unique, nor matter, can account for individuation. We therefore need to reason and reconstruct the logic of Plotinism in order to understand at what level individuation takes place.

Certainly, the logic of Plotinism leads us to believe that individuation is immediately determined by the diffusion of reasons, which are the bearers of the intelligible; we should therefore, in all rigor, consider that it is reasons that individuate and, at the same time, remember that reasons are only ever the development of intelligibles; consequently, we should deduce that if there is individuation, it can only be at the level of the latter. This is the thesis of the whole of Treatise 18, but also of Treatise 28, where, in chapter 5, Plotinus explains what it means to relate to oneself and to "possess oneself": basically, to know myself or to "relate to oneself" is to rediscover the reasons that have informed matter, reasons that themselves translate intelligibles; as a result, the self can only be played out at the level of being, and can only truly have meaning at the level of the fundamental structure of reality—i.e., at the level of reality. Hence Treatise 18, which asks whether there are forms of individual beings and responds favorably: "If I, and each of us, can be traced back to the intelligible, then the principle of each is also up there[82]." In this respect, by uniting with the Intellect, the soul does not dilute personal identity, but paradoxically discovers it at its source.

---

82. Plotinus, *Ennead* V, 7 [18], 1, 2-3, p. 409.

But let's never forget Plotinus' subtlety. Part of his genius consists in understanding that the question of individuation actually has two meanings, for on the one hand it involves that from which we come, the principle from which we are born and whose trace we keep, but on the other it involves the question of autonomy, and therefore of emancipation. If, in fact, there is a Form of individuals—let's call it "individuality"—then it belongs to the Intellect, hence to the second hypostasis, and will necessarily free itself from the latter. In this way, emancipation—that is, effective individuation— is deduced from the principle from which it comes, so that autonomy derives from the origin with which it breaks, which amounts to saying, as in the case of the soul's relationship to the Intellect, that the break is included in continuity. Therein lies the ambiguity of individuation, which at once makes sense only in the context of an intelligible Ego and, at the same time, is effectively individuated only in a singularization that obscures its ontological foundation.

3) The Beauty of Beauty

Incomplete would be an approach to Plotinus that avoided the difficult question of beauty and ugliness, which had a remarkable posterity in both the medieval and Renaissance worlds[83], and even in the revival of art history in the 20th century.[84]

In order to fully understand what follows, it is worth recalling a detail from the previous chapter, namely that the Good is defined as the supremely desirable; however, according to Plotinus' system, only one hypostasis can correspond to the Good, namely the One, as the supreme "reality" of the same nature as the Good; indeed, Treatise 33 affirms this self-evident fact that "whenever we speak of the 'One' and we speak of

---

83. For a first approach, we refer to Carole Talon-Hugon, *Une histoire personnelle et philosophique des arts*, tome II, *Moyen Âge et Renaissance*, Paris, PUF, 2014, in particular chapter 2: "Plotin et l'expérience esthétique".
84. See, for example, the importance given to it by Erwin Panofsky in *Idea*, cf. Erwin Panofsky, *Idea. Contribution à l'histoire du concept de l'ancienne théorie de l'art*, translation by Henri Joly, Paris, Gallimard, coll. Tel, 2003, especially pp. 41-48.

the 'Good', we must think of this nature and we must declare it to be 'one'[85]." The One as Good thus constitutes the supremely desirable, and "it is assuredly in the Good that is found what 'the soul pursues'; and that which supplies light to the Intellect, the slightest trace of it, by manifesting itself, arouses movement[86]." Now, of the One we have amply shown why we can say nothing; as a result, the One can only be associated with the Good from a perspective that does not really belong to it, which is that of desire, and which is therefore undoubtedly that of the soul ; to put it another way, *it seems that it is in the eyes of the soul that the One can be said to be Good*, and that for the soul, the Intellect itself, which comes from the One, seeks to know the One because, for it too, the latter is supremely desirable— and all desire of the Intellect is noetic desire; in short, the soul can affirm of the Intellect that it relates to the One as to the Good and that, making the One its object, it can in turn adopt the form of the Good. In short, the One "intelligentiates nothing, since it has nothing else

---

85. Plotinus, *Ennead* II, 9 [33], 1, 5-6, p. 201.
86. Plotinus, *Ennead* VI, 7 [38], 23, 1-2, p. 79.

to intelligentiate. Moreover, the Intellect is something other than the Good. Indeed, it takes the form of the Good, by virtue of the fact that it intelligentiates the Good[87]." Naturally, such a statement may come as a surprise in that, being beyond all being and therefore beyond all form, the One has no form at all—without which it would belong to the second hypostasis; This means that the One is grasped as the Good solely from the point of view of conversion, since every reality that attempts to return to the first hypostasis relates to it only insofar as it is desirable, and is therefore the supreme Good. We can therefore fix this first result: *in the perspective of conversion, the One takes the name of Good*, which it is not by itself, since otherwise the One would desire itself and would no longer be itself.

Once this has been established, the link with our purpose becomes clear: if all reality is turned by desire towards the supremely desirable, then all reality proceeds in one way or another from the One, and

---

87. Plotinus, *Ennead* V, 6 [24], 4, 4-6, p. 113.

their universal desire for the latter is the sign of this; consequently, "we must posit the Good as that to which all things are suspended, whereas it is suspended from nothing[88]". But let's draw the immediate consequence: if everything is suspended from the One, if "all things come from it[89]", then everything expresses at its level the radiance of the latter, and can be perceived as *beautiful*, beauty being the effective sign of the fact of being in one way or another part of the One. Beauty must therefore be conceived as the radiance of origin in all things, in differentiated ways, and this is the subject of the decisive Treatise 38 on questions relating to Beauty.[90]

We understand, then, that everything is beautiful insofar as everything proceeds from the One, and that the beauty of each level of being is the radiance conferred on it by the higher level, i.e. the principle.

---

88. Plotinus, *Ennead* I, 7 [54], 1, 21-22, p. 246.
89. Plotinus, *Ennead* VI, 7 [38], 23, 4-5, p. 79.
90. Pierre Hadot's commentary on this treatise is indispensable; cf. Plotinus, *Traité 38*, edited by Pierre Hadot, Paris, Cerf, 1987, republished by LGF, 1999.

To put it another way, the beautiful and the desirable are the same thing, and refer to the principle of each reality; thus, matter, which is as such formless and deprived of everything, desires Form, i.e. corporeity, and it is through corporeity as Form that it is beautiful, while the body, already informed, desires to find the principle diffusing the informing reasons, in this case the soul, and it is therefore through the soul that the body is beautiful. As for the soul, which comes from the Intellect, it desires the latter, and it is therefore the force that enables it to find it—virtue—that is beautiful. Finally, the Intellect desires the One, and is beautiful only through the form of the Good it knows[91]. Consequently, the beauty of each thing is an expression of the One in it, but also a desire for the latter, which is gradually fulfilled first by the desire for the principle immediately above.

This has two consequences. The first is that there are things that can be said to be "ugly", but nothing can be *absolutely* ugly, because absolute ugliness

---

91. This whole development is explained by Plotinus in *Ennead* VI, 7 [38], chap. 25, *passim.*

would be a *total* absence of Form, a kind of matter that has received no information, Plotinus evacuates this impossible situation in Treatise 54, making it clear that all things proceed from the One—including matter—because even things without souls are turned towards the latter, which in turn is turned towards the Intellect if it is virtuous, which itself relates to the One; as a result, "each possesses something of the Good, for each is 'one' in a certain way, just as it 'is' in a certain way. Each also still participates in a form[92]." But if absolute ugliness proves impossible, *relative* ugliness is quite conceivable when we are dealing with a body which, though informed, has matter that obscures form; "as for ugliness," writes Plotinus, "it is matter not dominated by form[93]". What does this mean? Not that there are bodies without Forms—that would be contradictory, since a body is defined as matter informed by reasons—but that the bodies that can be said to be ugly are those in which the structuring Form is not recognized. Ultimately, *an ugly body is one whose*

---

92. Plotinus, *Ennead* I, 7 [54], 2, 2-4, p. 246.
93. Plotinus, *Ennead* I, 8 [51], 5, 23, p. 46.

manifestation deviates materially from the corporeality that informs it.

The same applies to non-corporeal realities: a soul can be said to be ugly as long as it deviates from its principle, i.e. the Intellect. To deviate from its principle is to adopt the view we described earlier, and to allow oneself to be seduced by matter as matter, while at the same time allowing oneself to be affected by the soul's multiple affections. The "ugly soul[94]" is therefore the weak soul that strays from itself—and therefore from its principle—and allows itself to flow towards "mortal and base objects of thought[95]" out of weakness. The ugliness of the soul is thus never more than the weakness of the soul that distances it from its own reality—that is, from the Intellect that gives it its radiance.

The second consequence is that beauty is no longer so much a matter of mathematical structure—proportion—as of the brilliance or resplendence of the

---

94. Plotinus, *Ennead* I, 6 [1], 5, 26, p. 73.
95. *Ibid.*

principle from which the reality we are dealing with derives. The beautiful Greek proportion thus loses its aesthetic privilege to what Plotinus calls "radiant objects[96]", which express adequacy to their own nature—and therefore to their principle, for which reason the principle is the very source of their beauty. This gave rise to an aesthetic of light and lightning, rather than of harmonious structure, which is sustained by the very emergence of Form from matter, and from which the Renaissance was to make the most of; consider Michelangelo and his desire to make the body protrude from matter, as if to extract from it the process of informing matter and forming bodies, exhibiting the intelligible principle from which reasons derive[97].

---

96. *Ibid*, 9, 2, p. 78.

97. On the Plotinian source of Renaissance art, see Erwin Panofsky, *Essais d'iconologie,* translation by Claude Herbette and Bernard Teyssedre, Paris, Gallimard, 1967, especially chapters V and VI, and Thibaut Gress, *L'œil et l'intelligible*, tome II, *Essai sur le sens philosophique de la forme en peinture*, Paris, Kimé, 2015, especially pp. 239-250 and 461-500.

Conclusion: Plotinus' Continuism and the Will of the One

Understanding Plotinus therefore involves a dual effort, both intellectual and sensory. It involves determining the meaning of concepts, but also feeling that the world as it appears to us expresses much more than itself, and even constitutes an invitation to the soul's conversion to Intellect. If I fail to see in a majestic oak tree the marvellous radiance of its Form, I miss the meaning of the world and stray from the very reality of all things.

The latter are part of a perpetually dynamic and ever-changing scheme in which, starting from the One, a series of realities are generated that functionally aspire to find their origin. Indeed, if the One in some way causes itself—although this is already saying too much—and then causes the Intellect, which causes the soul, which causes matter and bodily forms organized via reasons, then a kind of chain of being is established that ultimately aspires to only one thing: to turn towards the supreme and supremely desirable Origin, namely the One conceived as Good. This entire series constitutes a procession, that is, an unfolding of the One that manifests through this ontological and material bouquet its superabundance, its excess towards itself, through which it strangely gives what it does not have. The One is that reality which overflows itself, and out of which proceed beings in series, situated at differentiated levels and aspiring to convert in stages towards their unique origin.

Plotinus' ontology is, for the reason mentioned, profoundly *continuistic*: from the One to matter, there are no breaks or leaps, but a series of begats of realities which, by virtue of their very perfection, overflow themselves, become producers and are transmitted from one to the next as far as matter. Realities are no longer separate from one another, but extend one another, each being the effect of the perfection of the superior reality.

It is then possible to grasp again the whole of what we have analyzed in a new way: the movement out of the One, called procession (*proodos*), responds to the very necessity of the nature of perfect entities. It is in their nature to transmit their own perfection outside themselves, and autarky therefore seems contrary to the very idea of perfection. Thus, from the One *proceeds* the Intellect, the level of intelligible realities and thought, which in turn overflows itself by causing the soul, which engenders matter and bodies. All this is like a diffusion of the One in concentric circles, producing a number of effects that are increasingly indirect, but which nonetheless provide an increasingly approximate image of the One.

Nevertheless, procession cannot be thought of in isolation: if it is the nature of perfect realities to diffuse out of themselves, it is the function of begotten beings to rediscover their origin, to return to the source from which they proceed. This conversion, inscribed in the very nature of all things, calls for a final clarification: *the Intellect is truly the Intellect only when it turns towards the One, just as the soul is truly the soul only when it turns towards the Intellect.* Derivative realities actualize their being only when they turn by conversion towards their source: a non-thinking soul thus remains a potential soul, just as a body distanced from the soul would sink into formless ugliness. And perhaps we can even go so far as to say, by virtue of Treatise 30, that a body is only a body if it is natural, and therefore only if it contemplates the soul of the world, through which it will ascend, step by step, to the One.

Plotinism must therefore be imagined as a *dynamic ontology* in which realities are generated from all eternity, move away from each other by procession and move towards each other by conversion: there is a *beating of* the world in Plotinus, a *rhythm* by which realities expand and contract—these are only spatial metaphors, not rigorous descriptions—diffuse and return to their origin. This is very apparent to us humans, when we examine our behavior: We can sometimes become dispersed, attracted by the multiplicity of matter, in which case the soul, out of weakness, finds itself as if magnetized by material dispersion. But we can also become concentrated, i.e. turn in on ourselves and thus tear ourselves away from the temptation of the multiple to become one with ourselves; it is then that we can think, and tear ourselves away from our particularity to go back to universal, eternally true, unchanging realities, and thus rediscover the Intellect. Only then can the soul be said to be beautiful, and an obvious complicity be established between beauty and interiority[98].

Plotinus calls this back-and-forth movement out of and towards the One *life*[99]. This in no way refers to

---

98. "[...] for yourself, remove the superfluous, straighten what is twisted and, purifying all that is tenebrous, work to be resplendent. Do not cease to sculpt your own statue until the splendor of virtue shines in you and you see temperance sitting on its 'august throne'", Plotinus, *Ennead* I, 6 [1], 9, 10-15, p. 79.

99. Cf on this subject Pierre Hadot, "Être, vie, pensée chez Plotin et avant Plotin", in *Plotin. Porphyre. Études néoplatoniciennes*, Paris, Les Belles Lettres, 1999 and Benard Collette-Dučić, *Plotin et l'ordonnancement de l'être*, Paris, Vrin, 2007, pp. 70-73 [check pagination?].

biological life, but rather to the pulsation of realities outside the First Principle. Life is therefore the radiation from the One through which realities dynamically generate themselves and seek the source from which they originate: this vital, living movement is crystallized to the full in thought, which is then the radiation of the One, its vital dynamization in which otherness, movement and infinity are found. The Intellect is in fact dual, since the intelligé differs from the intelligeant; it is movement, since it animates thought; and it is infinite, since it is eternal and greater than any number.

Joachim Lacrosse writes: "Levels of intellection are as many kinds of life, differentiated according to their relative clarity. These different lives, these different intellections, are *logoi*, reasons or expressions that manifest in their own register, the intellect's relationship to itself[100]."

---

100. Joachim Lacrosse, *op. cit.* p. 114.

Thus, true life is first and foremost intellectual, a movement through which thought sets itself in motion and seeks to return to its primordial origin. This is the essence of Plotinism: *thought exists only because there is a loss of the One and a desire to return to it.* In other words, if we humans are not content with purely material life, it's not out of whim, but out of nostalgia for the origin, to use Ferdinand Alquié's words: something at the heart of our singularity reminds us of where we come from, and invites us to turn away from material bodies and concentrate on our soul, to go back to the Intellect; but *thinking is not enough*, intellectual life is not the last word in Plotinism, although it is its central activity; *intellectual life exists only because there is a will to rediscover the One*, so that each level of intellection designates a level of life whose ultimate purpose is paradoxically to lead us out of life, i.e. towards the One.

Better still: since the One "wants to be itself[101]", or that "its will and itself are one[102]", it's a safe bet that the

---

101. Plotinus, *Ennead* VI, 8 [39], 13, 29, p. 227.
102. Ibid, 13, 30, p. 227.

will that drives us to convert to the One *is* the latter's will to grasp itself, and that the whole procession we've described is nothing but the Origin's effort to finally know itself.

Table of Contents

Best sellers Max Milo Editions

Hitler's banker, Jean-François Bouchard

Confessions of a forger, Éric Piedoie Le Tiec

The Koran and the flesh, Ludovic-Mohamed Zahed

Governing by fake news, Jacques Baud

Governing by chaos, Collectif

A political history of food, Paul Ariès

Mad in U.S.A.: The ravages of the "American model",
Michel Desmurget

Mondial soccer club geopolitics, Kévin Veyssière

Putin: Game master?, Jacques Baud

Treatise on the three impostors: Moses, Jesus, Muhammad,
The Spirit of Spinoza

TV Lobotomy, Michel Desmurget

The Russian Art of war, Jacques Baud